Choices in the Afterlife

by

Gretchen Vogel

May you find some comfort here,

Gretchen

Choices Publishing SAN: 856-3616
Choices Publishing
Po Box 222
Keene, NH 03431
ChoicesPublishing@mail.com
www.HowSpiritWorks.com

Second Edition April 2010
ISBN 0-9766779-0-3
978-0-9766779-0-1

Choices in the Afterlife

What we can do
and
Where we can go after death

www.HowSpiritWorks.com

OTHER BOOKS BY GRETCHEN VOGEL

Solar Gardening

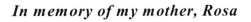

In memory of my mother, Rosa

Contents

Appendices

Foreword

A friend once joked with me that I look forward to the afterlife like some people look forward to retirement. I know where I will go when this life ends and what I will choose to do. I know what will be possible for me and what won't be possible anymore. I don't *want* to die. The earth is beautiful and life is a gift. But I know when my death comes I won't be frightened. I don't want you to be frightened either.

The reason I'm not afraid of death is because, for more than two decades, I have been able to communicate with the deceased. I discovered this ability while praying for deceased loved ones. Often, when I prayed for my paternal grandmother, she seemed to be with me. I thought this was just a comforting hallucination until she began to tell me things that I could not have known. When things she told me proved true, I began to think something unusual was happening. I started to experiment for friends and acquaintances with their deceased loved ones. I gradually found myself working with people all over the country.

Through prayer and meditation techniques, I ask to be with a chosen deceased individual. Most of the time I can tune into them much like finding a signal on a radio. In my mind I can see the deceased, their gestures, clothing and facial expressions. I also see a scene where we meet. This can be a natural setting, a park, or a room within a house. I can describe these scenes in detail. The living people I am working for recognize the location I describe. Often the smallest thing, such as a piece of jewelry the deceased is wearing, or some small, seemingly insignificant gesture is the most compelling proof to the living of their deceased loved one's survival.

In my mind I can also hear the thoughts the deceased individuals are projecting to me. I put their thoughts and ideas into words and speak them into a tape recorder. The deceased often have something specific they want to convey to their living loved ones. The messages don't have to make sense to me. I am only the medium through which this event takes place. But healing happens. Grief is eased.

The living people I work for treasure the details and special phrases that indicate their loved ones still exist. But early on I became fascinated by the similarities between different deceased people's experiences. My compassion for the pain of separation between the living and the deceased kept me doing this work. But the work evolved into my passion to understand this next reality. After all, this would be my reality one day too.

Polls show most of us believe our deceased loved ones still exist in some form or place. It is possible for the deceased to show us they survived death in many ways. They can enhance the blooms of favorite flowers, flowering bushes or trees. They demonstrate their presence when we smell their pipe smoke or perfume out of the blue. The deceased can also reach us when we are dreaming. Electronic devices such as lights or telephones can easily be influenced by the deceased.

Whether we believe our loved ones survived their death doesn't matter. They did. Whether we believe we will survive our death also doesn't matter. We will. All of us can have some understanding of how the afterlife will be.

If you asked twenty people to describe life to you there would be twenty different perspectives. Parents might bring up their children first, children might talk about their toys, friends or pets, adults may focus on their career or home. The core of life for the elderly may be their physical challenges.

When I asked each deceased person I contacted how they perceived the afterlife I heard many different opinions and interpretations. Everyone's story of how they left their body or experienced death, achieved consciousness out of body, how they healed and chose meaningful activities in their new reality was unique. But I began to understand there was a general pattern to the after death experience. I saw a progression of choices and experiences within the individual's stories.

I became able to describe the afterlife in two ways. One way was in terms of what the deceased chose to do and the second way is where they chose to do it.

I had much to learn from the deceased before I could share information with or help anyone, living or dead. I learned, for example, the afterlife is a completely self directed mental and spiritual reality. We still have free will and make choices in the afterlife. We do have help. We can ask the predeceased who greet us and/or other guides to inform us, but our choices are our own. No exact pattern exists for everyone, and each deceased can have a somewhat different subjective experience of the afterlife.

In my study of death, I have also come to understand our experience as self knowing individuals takes place on more than just the surface of the earth. Our journey starts from God/Source and brings us into denser and denser energy levels. The choice to be a human leads to a pre-birth focus and our first lifetime in physical form on earth. Death begins our afterlife and is the start of a journey outward into less dense and increasingly less tangible yet more energized levels of experience. As individuals we can wave in and out of lifetimes, in fact most of us do reincarnate. Our lifetimes on earth are brief yet incredibly important learning opportunities within our soul's long evolution.

The single most profound thing I learned from my work with the deceased is that no one outside the self who judges us after death. We are the judge and jury of our own life choices.

In life we can seek the knowledge to make choices that enlighten, heal and progress our body, mind and spirit. Alternatively, we can make the choice to not learn from our mistakes and make our life worse and worse. This way of life narrows our choices by fostering ignorance. Some people devote their time here to evil in repetitive destructive acts and create profound ignorance within themselves. Ignorance of choice limits the possibilities both in physical life and in the afterlife.

Heavens and hells exist but they are the heavens and hells of our own making. We create our own individual heaven or hell on earth with our choices and how we think about life. We begin experience in the afterlife with the same thought processes, the same attitudes, beliefs and awareness but without a physical body.

Chapter One

The Definitions of Death

Death is mysterious
because we don't understand
what happens when someone dies.

I am as dazed and saddened as anyone else when someone I love dies. Being able to contact someone I love, mentally, is no substitute for a hug, laughing over a joke or fixing them dinner. I cling as strongly as anyone to the tangible symbols of our previously shared life. When I visit my mother's grave, I trace the fact of her death carved in the headstone. I try to comprehend that the bones she once walked with now lie beneath the earth.

I keep the urn with the ashes of my first Labrador Retriever in my office. I cling to what little remains of him here. I miss and grieve my deceased loved ones as much as you do. Death is just not a mystery to me.

To the living, death seems to be completely about the physical body. The medical profession defines death as the cessation of brain, heart or lung function. A profound change in a body occurs at death; an animated body becomes inanimate.

It is natural for us to associate the deceased person with the physical remains of their body. The wake, funeral and burial rites are centered around the body or ashes of a friend or loved one. These rituals are necessary for our grieving process even though it is clear the body is only a symbol of the person who was once there.

Matter can neither be created nor destroyed. After death the water and minerals that make up the physical body will be dispersed or recycled in the natural decay process. The energy that makes up the personality shifts in the death transition. This does not mean that the personality goes up, down or sideways. It just means

3

there is a change in energy. The energy situation that people find themselves in after death may be a higher or better state because they are no longer encumbered by their physical body. We cannot perceive the personality's transition with our physical senses even if we are in the same room with them when they die. Our misconceptions about death are logical ones.

The death of a friend or family member is an event to the living. But death is more of a process for the deceased. They see their death as a transition from physical reality to a different reality. To them, along with the dropping or falling away of the physical body, death is their transformation to a new state or a new stage of existence.

No matter what causes the death, no matter what the experience is of dying, death is a transition. Before death we are in the physical world with this particular density of energy. After death our personality continues in another plane of energy. The transition itself is death-and not what comes after it. In our language and physical viewpoint, death and being dead may be the same thing. But we are not in that transition forever.

No one set way to experience the transition of death exists. I cannot say there is one way to die, any right way to die. Some people are conscious throughout this transition. Others may only remember their death after searching their memory when they "wake up" in a different reality. Some people prepare for death as they age, others are ambushed by tragic, unexpected deaths.

I chose the stories of three unexpected deaths from my meditations for this chapter. I must first explain these scenes and conversations are all taking place in my mind. When I meditate, I pray, dedicating my work for good and to God. I visualize a small image of myself on an open flower in the center of my head. I then ask my angels for protection as I follow a path out from my head to a scene where I meet the deceased. I am the one traveling to them, but it is moving to a different energy level with my mind. I test the validity of what I mentally see with the white light of God's love. What I speak into the tape recorder is a combination of what I mentally hear and also words that I assign to what the deceased are communicating to me. Mental communication with the deceased happens quickly. The scenes they show me and the thoughts or ideas they convey in a split second can take me over a minute to speak. When the communication is over, I follow the path back to my body.

The first meditation I want to share with you is with Norma. Norma was an official in a town where I once lived. She died of heart failure on Christmas Eve. This rocked our small community as she was admired and loved by many. Norma had been deceased for six months when I did this work.

In meditation I asked to be with Norma. I had the visualization of a reddish orange recliner through a window in the upper half of a door. I knocked and asked her if I might come in. She got up and came to greet me and we hugged. I pulled up a wooden chair with a braided rug seat cushion facing her. I asked Norma's permission to throw the white light, symbolizing God's love toward her to make sure the image I had of her in my mind was true.

As the light washed and sparkled around her she receded a little bit. I had the sense she was fearful. She said, "nothing like this has happened to me here." I assured her she was in control, that our conversation didn't have to be any more personal than she wanted it to be. I told her I was doing this work with other deceased townspeople when she knew me in life. I just didn't tell many people what I did. I reassured Norma she did not have to be afraid of my influence, and if I asked her something she didn't want to answer, it was no problem. She laughed and said how easy going I was when she knew me in life. Then, in a few seconds I caught her up on my life since we last saw each other.

I commented to her on the floating quality of the body she is projecting to me; that I see her in. She was a large woman in life and her memory body is also large. She said, "it is not difficult for me to move around now. I move from place to place and it amazes me still how easy it is. Getting around in life was such a big effort."

I asked her if she was aware of her funeral. The little church was packed with people who loved you, with people you had helped. She said, "Things were not clear to me yet. I did perceive what was going on but it was through a fog. There was so much grief coming from my family that I couldn't be right there in all that emotion. All that emotion created a barrier between me and my family. I wasn't really sure where I was at that point."

6

"The house itself (meaning the house she lived in until she died) is where I spend most of my time now. It is empty and feels like a protective shell to me. I still watch out the windows and have privacy. This is where I got back the feeling of being myself."

I asked Norma what the experience of her death was like. She answered, "I was afraid when I died because I was by myself, I was alone. It felt like drowning. I tried to stay in my body for my family, so my transition was not quick. I was not confused but I was trying to use my will to stay alive."

"Eventually I did feel warmth and the absence of pain. When I realized it was inevitable I did move toward the light. On the way I passed Jack (her predeceased husband). He looked so solid to me, exactly as he would have in life, while everything else around me was less defined, softer looking. But he was really solid. We didn't communicate but he watched me move up higher toward the light."

"I had a strong sense that my ancestors were beyond Jack, closer to the point of light. I had the feeling of coming home to them. The family on the other side almost balanced, in a way, the family I was leaving behind. It was a joyful concept to me that I could be with my parents again. We had a reunion for a while."

"At first they seemed to be just formless shapes. As I stayed with them, I was able to see more of their clothing and what they looked like. I didn't question going beyond or back, I just stayed with them for the time it took for me to become oriented to the other side."

I asked Norma where they are now. She answered, "they are further up than I am. They are beyond the tunnel. (By tunnel she means the earth portal.) I know I can go visit them in my mind, but it is more like a telephone call now than actually being with them. Jack calls me in that same way. I have not been where he is, in his presence, since I died."

She continued, "I am very busy observing my family here on the earth, making sure the (grand) kids get to school safely. I still go to church with everyone." Norma attended the little Catholic church in our town, and by everyone she means the living who are going to church. She continued," I think it is important for me to keep prayer in my life (she means her afterlife). I even have time now to say the whole rosary. Before, I'd get about three Hail Marys in and the phone would ring."

"I wish I could reassure my children of my love and my presence. Even in dream state they still don't quite believe we are together..." Norma and I then took a few minutes to gossip about the people in the town we both knew and loved. After that Norma began to talk about her life.

She said, "I got involved with being a town official because I had a keen sense of what was right and what was wrong. I knew what was possible for people and what wasn't. It is not good for a person to hold office and be in power if they haven't had to make supper with just what they had in the house. Someone who is wealthy, and has never had to scratch out a meal for their family, just won't know what it is like for other people."

"I also liked the ritual of the meetings. The town meetings, the elections, and even the selectmen's meetings were all a process that was very ritualistic. I liked recording people's everyday lives, things that were not important to anyone else but those individuals. And the parts of the work that became the town history were important. I left a lot of signatures on an awful lot of documents that are in the town hall. So much of it was really just mundane events but things that affected individual people's lives."

"I miss it. I would have liked to have stayed (alive) there and been healthy. I enjoyed my days. I was not a depressed person. If I didn't seem enthusiastic at times it was because I wasn't feeling well. I feel healthy now and I am in no hurry to move on."

Norma was kind to everyone in town, but I really appreciated her kindness to me during a hard part of my life. I transferred as much love and light as I could as my way of thanking her for her support when she was alive and for meeting with me now.

Charlene was a close friend when we were young teenagers. I moved away before college but we always kept in touch with a few cards or phone calls each year. Charlene died suddenly in middle age of a heart attack. Her partner told me she had been resuscitated and at one point had even started breathing on her own. But she couldn't be saved. This is a part of a meditation with Charlene just a week after her death.

After praying I followed a pathway in my mind that led to a grove of trees under lit by the reflection of light on water. I sensed this was near Lake Erie. There are picnic tables here and charcoal grills mounted on metal pipes. I saw an image of Charlene walking toward me. Her hair is blowing slightly in the breeze and she is wearing shorts, a sleeveless blouse and sandals. I asked to test her image with white light and as I throw the light toward her she thinks she is going to get wet. We laughed. She thought this would feel like the bucket of ice water that is thrown over the coach at ball games.

We continued to move closer until we were able to embrace. There was a welling of emotion in us both. We were happy to see each other but there was a lot of sadness at the same time. We sat on the benches of a picnic table facing each other. I told her, I want to hear what you are thinking and feeling if you want to share that with me.

She said, "I loved my life. I knew I loved it when I was in it, but I never knew how much until I lost it. (I loved) even the not so great things like driving to work in bad weather or the gray days. I'd give anything to have them back. I miss so much the ordinary parts of life like buying dog food, cleaning the garage, the most mundane and unappealing parts of life. I can't even think about the good things I miss yet. I never thought I'd miss going to work, it was so boring, I'd give anything to walk through those doors again." We then hold hands across the table and she is crying.

She continued, "I can't believe I am at this level of emotion. It is overwhelming because I was never this sad in life. I never got this down. Sure there were rough spots but I never felt despair like this before."

10

was not married at the time of her death but she must have been planning her marriage. I got the sense that her family buried her in her wedding dress.) "I really don't know for how long. I kept expecting to wake up and it would all be a dream. I thought I was dreaming, and thought if I stayed with my body that it would just get up and move on and not be dead or underground. I thought then I could get on with my life. I stayed with my body in the coffin for what turned out to be several months."

"When it was spring above the ground (she died in the winter) it made me want to get up and wake up. I sensed the flowers bursting forth and all the life above the ground. It was wonderful to be around the flowers. I experienced being lighter than when I was in my body."

"I stayed with the unfolding of spring for a while. I moved slowly and still felt sleepy. I learned I did not have a physical body when my family came to visit the grave. I'd walk right through them, I would hug them and they wouldn't know I was there. I did not feel dead, but I could not get them to hear me when I talked to them."

"All that summer I just stayed close to my grave and watched the season. Then I tentatively began to wander around. I finally made it back to the farm. I stayed there and just sat in the house. I thought about what had happened during my life and would relive certain times I had in that house. I saw how sad my parents were and that made me just cry and cry with them."

"Then one of my brothers got married and had a child. When I saw that baby being born that released me from being near the earth. I began to understand things on a more cosmic level then. After that I was propelled to another place that was just a kaleidoscope of colors. There, I learned to be happy again. I splashed and played, but I was still by myself. I stayed there until I felt like being around people and doing things again."

Once Norma, Charlene and Ann realized they were still themselves, although out of their physical body, mentally their death transition was complete. Norma knew what was happening right away. Charlene faced her new reality within days, and Ann took some months to understand she had died. They all had to realize they were now outside, but alongside of the physical experience.

This brings us to yet another definition of death. Death can also be defined for the deceased in a subjective way. For the deceased, death is when they learn they are dead. Choices in the afterlife cannot be made until we know we are dead.

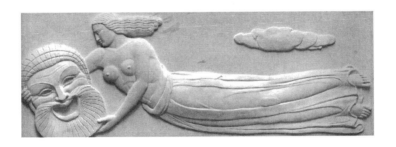

Chapter Two

Self Realization

Self realization is not learned by dying.
It is developed in life.

What would your answer be if you were asked: who are you? Not what is your name or what you do for work, not who is your family, not where do you live, but who are you? You could begin to answer this question by thinking of who you are physically, mentally and spiritually. The question really is: who are you right now? You wouldn't answer the question with who you were as a child or who you might be in old age.

It is important to understand who we are in physical life because it begins to answer the question of who we are in the afterlife. The better we understand who and what we are here the better we can understand who and what we will be in the afterlife. Physical life has to be the starting point to explain how we exist in the afterlife.

How we would define our self should not be such a tough question. How could we not know our self in life? After all we are with our self all day long. But we might also wonder how could we not know our self in the afterlife. After death we'll still be our self.

On earth, we are the combination of body, mind and spirit. This is the first part of self realization. The other part of self realization is understanding that we are in our present all the time. Even though we may be thinking about the past, or planning for the future, we are all and always only in one place - the present. So, right now you are the combination of body, mind and spirit, in your present, reading this book.

However, what the self consists of, or is made up of, changes somewhat in the death transition. Self realization in the afterlife is understanding we are the combination of mind and spirit without the physical body. The major change at death is obviously the dropping of the physical body. Many other things do not change at death. For example, our personality does not change. The fact that we are in our present does not change.

This second element to self realization, understanding that we can only exist in our very own present is really important in the afterlife. Sometimes the deceased do not know that they are dead because they do not know they are still in their present. Some deceased feel they are dreaming that they are dead, especially in the case of an unexpected or sudden death. Other deceased never lose consciousness during the death transition. These deceased know they are dead because they remember the event of their death as something that happened in the recent past.

I would like to share with you my meditation with Chris. She had easily achieved self realization after death even though she told me that she had not been a spiritual person in life. Chris was the mother of young children and also a science teacher. She continues to teach us with these words shared with me about a year after her death in a violent accident.

Chris said, "Even though I am deceased, my (memory) body feels as real to me as yours does to you. I know how to move around. I take walks on the beach. I curl up in my favorite chair at home. I can feel the beauty around me. Now I have time to look at the things

I didn't have time for before, like the birds at the bird feeder (at her home)."

"My vision is not dependent on light. If I will myself to see the way I did with my eyes, I can perceive what is in front of me. Seeing a sunset, for example, is more knowing what the sunset looks like than what it was actually like to look at it with my eyes."

"The information comes into my mind in a different way. When I was in my (physical) body the light from an object or scene was reflected in through my eyes, my optic nerves to my brain. This activated a chemical reaction that told me what I was looking at. I will still get the same information from what I focus on, but the information comes directly into my mind instead of through my eyes. My mental perception is as accurate as if I was seeing it with my eyes."

"But this kind of seeing affects me a lot less than eyesight did. Without a body to take care of and watch out for, the accuracy of my perception is not that important. I'm not worried about tripping over something or falling off something."

"It is the strangest thing just to walk through doors, people and buildings as if they are air. I tend to stay on the ground most of the time. But walking through walls still makes me feel like Superman."

"When my (still living) husband is frying bacon I can remember what bacon smelled like. When it burns or just begins to cook I can experience that through my memory. It feels like sensory input into my body. I feel like I am smelling the bacon although I can't be smelling it the way I did when I was alive. I remember the aroma so accurately that this sense does seem the same to me."

"The one sense I don't seem to have any more is the sense of touch. When I put what I think of as my hand into fire or snow I don't feel anything. It is hard for me to convince myself that this is hot, or this is cold. Of all the 'senses' now that I am deceased, touch is the least realistic. I can remember what something felt like when I touched it in life but it takes a real effort. If I concentrate, I can sustain the memory for a few moments."

"I can experience taste somewhat, by being near someone who is eating, more directly than I can smell things now. But I don't hang around pizza or ice cream parlors 'tasting' things randomly because I would pick up on thoughts or vibes from strangers that I don't want to feel or know. So I taste only with my own family when they are eating.

"I hear things because of the vibration that sound makes. I suppose this is because sound makes air molecules move. I can hear people talking clearly. I seek out concerts because I still enjoy music so much. Of all the senses, hearing is the one that is most like it was when I was in a body. The sound is picked up all over my (memory) body now. I think this must be how a deaf person feels, picking up the vibrations of music through the floor or through the air. I am grateful I can still enjoy music. I feel the music in the air."

Chris is in her present and functioning well without her physical body. In life it is natural for us to identify ourselves primarily with our physical body. Our senses: sight, touch, hearing, taste, and smell, are the way we interpret reality, the way we experience life. We rely on our body to carry us through life.

One of the first steps to understand how we survive death is to think of the physical body as a vehicle of our self. The body is taken up by the personality at birth and is left in the physical world at death. I don't mean we should relate to our body the same way we would to a car. We are stewards of our body and it is in our self interest to treat our body with respect.

We tend to think we are our body in life. But the body we have is a temporary vehicle. Over a lifetime the materials that make up our body change several times. Every cell in the body is gradually, yet completely replaced every seven to ten years. So the physical substance that makes up our body is different at the approximate ages of seven, fourteen, twenty one and so on. We can think of this as having several different bodies over the course of our life.

The body I have now only remotely resembles the body I had as a teenager. I feel like I am only impersonating a middle age woman. It wasn't until my parents were in their mid eighties that they seemed old to me. Their physical limitations bewildered them because they thought they should still be able to do much of what they used to. Our personality, our consistent sense of our self, does not change as dramatically as our body does in the course of a lifetime. This is because our personality is contained or carried in our mind.

Many people think of brain function and the mind as being the same thing. So how could the personality survive the death of our brain? The brain monitors the working systems of the human body. The brain's job is to keep the body alive. The brain is an organ in the body that regulates the nervous system. We perceive our world primarily through the sensory input of the nervous system. So it is hard to understand the self in any other way than through the nervous system's interpretation of reality. It is a logical conclusion that the brain must also be the seat of the mind. It isn't.

If we had to think of a place in our physical body where the mind is, the spinal cord would be a more logical location. This is because the spine is the pathway for all energy flows in the nervous system. Ancient tradition describes a column of energy from the base of our spine to the top of our head. This traditional understanding describes the mind's metaphorical location in the body.

I began to understand the difference between mind and brain function when I started to do my work as a medium. At first I could be with the deceased in my mind. But I could not make the connection between my mental vision and the speech part of my brain. Once I learned to bridge that gap I could speak what I was "seeing" and "hearing" into a tape recorder. If you saw me deep in a meditative state, you would see me drink tea, scratch my toes, and even walk around. What is happening with my body, thirst, an itch or the need to move around is my brain directing me. What is happening in the meditation is the working of my mind. Everyone in life is functioning with both their mind and their brain.

Another way to see the difference between mind and brain is in a brain injured individual. A friend, Nan, sustained a brain injury in an auto accident. Before the accident she was quite smart. After, she struggled with the sequence of actions necessary to make coffee. Nan's mind and soul haven't changed, though she now has to express her self through a flawed vehicle. Anyone who works with the brain injured knows that the personality is still inside there, coping as best they can.

If brain function and the mind's intent were not different, they could not be at odds with each other. Depression is a common biological condition. Certain brain chemicals become deficient and the depressed person can feel this biology as their reality. What tragic ramifications brain chemistry can have on the personality! People commit suicide. A person's opportunities for learning and completing their life's intent on earth is destroyed.

Most women eventually learn not to take the hormonal changes within their body too seriously as the hormones affect their emotions and their thinking. Women learn there are better times of the month than others to make major life decisions. Another hormone driven brain chemistry phenomena is lust. This biological response is often confused with love. But unconditional love comes from the mind and has nothing to do with hormones.

When we concentrate on anything, we exercise our mind. In school, we first learn and practice concentration. Memories are reached through concentration. Concentration is the gateway to tap into our mind's intuition and creativity.

People who believe mind is literally linked to brain function are at a disadvantage when contemplating death. If self-knowing is achieved only through that one organ, the brain, how could we know our self after death? In truth, the mind interacts with the physical body but the mind survives the death of the physical body.

A personality enters the dance of physical life at birth and exits the physical body at death. Mind carries our identity, what makes our personality unique. Mind contains memory, the sense of self, and creativity. The mind can overrule the brain and is primarily what drives our actions; makes our choices. All that we do in life is held in our mind as memory. Everything the mind contains: our personality, memories, knowledge, intuition, attitudes, beliefs and creativity, are carried, in our mind, into the afterlife.

At our very core, however, we are spirit or soul. Through our religions we learn that the spiritual nature of the living human being is not linked or bound in the physical body. It is, therefore, easy to understand that the soul or spirit continues beyond death. What this implies though is the soul or spirit does not include the mind. This is a misconception because mind and spirit are entwined throughout life and the afterlife.

All of us, everything that exists came from the vast, incomprehensible energy: God/Source. Everything that exists was a part of God/Source before it existed. Every rock, tree, insect, animal and human, planet, and galaxy carry inherently within it the initial component of

God/Source which blossomed into a rock, tree, insect, animal, human, star or planet. This distilled God/Source component is how we are all the same.

It is hard for us to grasp the concept of this sameness. It would be like seeing a whole different energy behind what we are looking at. What if you were looking at a scene containing a building, the sidewalk, power lines, people walking pets, trees and bushes, and you comprehended all this not as the physical substance, but just for a moment, as iridescent starlight in the shape of the physical objects still in motion and in time. Then you might get a glimpse of this concept of the underlying essential sameness of everything.

I link the two words, God and Source, because we have to assign words to the origin of creation. I have no wish to challenge anyone's religious metaphors. All religions contain truth. In the simplest of terms, we come from God/Source. Our long journey culminates in our final physical lifetime, and our ultimate goal is to return to God/Source.

Our spiritual nature endows the personality with the ability to draw in, draw on, and amplify God/Source energy. We nurture this core aspect of our personality by first acknowledging that we are, in part, spirit. And then like a leaf absorbing sunlight, we can draw on God/Source energy, or grace, to enhance our experience on earth. Love is the key. When we are capable of unselfish love, we draw in God/Source energy. When we focus love on anything else, we are passing this energy on.

Spiritual practices such as kindness, prayer and meditation are the way we focus and exercise this aspect of our personality. The deceased, to the extent that they are aware of their spiritual nature, continue to enhance their spiritual experience in the afterlife. We do not begin the afterlife as a different spiritual person than we were when we died. As one person expressed in one of my meditations, "death is not the ticket to enlightenment; enlightenment happens in life if it is to happen at all." Loving, light filled, prayerful people in life are still devoted, loving people as they embark on their afterlife.

I saw a similarity between the way the deceased relate to their reality structure after death and the way we consider our reality in life. Many deceased don't question the fact that they feel as if they are still in a body. They don't wonder at their ability to think, remember and communicate even though they no longer have a physical brain. Many deceased I have communicated with said that they still pray.

Many of us don't question the meaning of the physical body. We don't see it as a tool for learning, or as a vehicle for the personality. We are just in it. The time most people ponder their essential nature is when they are approaching death.

Chapter Three

Approaching Death

Death is held as such a mystery that the only time most people embark on the voyage of self realization is when they are faced with the inevitability of their death.

I've been working on this book, on and off, for more than a decade. As the book really began to come together, several people asked me who my market was for the book. I am amused by that question because everyone who will die is my market for this book. Perhaps there are some of us who are not planning to die. They won't need to know how the afterlife will be. The rest of us can be somewhat prepared for our death transition and less fearful as we approach our death.

One way we can prepare for death is to become self aware, or work at self realization in life. The key to self realization in life was discussed in the last chapter. It is understanding our self as the combination of body, mind, and spirit in our present physical experience. The word personality also helps us understand what, of our self, survives physical death. Personality is defined as the qualities that form an individual's character.

One of my goals for this book is to express how the personality continues in the afterlife. Death does not change that essence of us. Our personality continues to evolve with the same attitudes, or feelings about things, that governed our choices in life. The choices we make in the afterlife resonate with the themes of our life.

In so many of the meditations with the deceased I got a feeling for who they were in life. I got a feeling for their personality from what they chose to talk with me about. The things that were important to them after death reflected their personality and their attitudes about life. That outlook on life carried over to their choices in the afterlife.

I once did a meditation for a friend who suspected someone from the afterlife was trying to reach him. My friend had a small table in his house, covered with more than a dozen photos of friends and relatives. One day when he came home from work every single photo was turned face down except one. He thought the cat might have done this, except the next morning a candle in a wall holder (out of reach of the cat) was tipped toward one side. He could allow the wall had been knocked somehow, and the candle tilted. But that night when he came home from work, the candle was out of the holder and laying, as if placed, on an open shelf in the sideboard nearby. I was at a party, at his house, a week or so later and he said he had something to ask me. Before we got a chance to talk, I felt an incredible energy coming from a photo of his stepmother on a small table nearby. It was the only photo, I learned later, that the cat(?) had left still standing. I was then pretty sure I knew who was trying to reach him. A few days after the party, I sat in meditation to communicate with her.

Cathy was so close to me, so focused on me, that as soon as I opened my mind in meditation she was there. I asked her to create a place where we could sit and talk. She visualized a room and I (mentally) sat on a couch. Cathy sat in one of the wing chairs flanking an ornamental fireplace. Between us was a coffee table with an ashtray and a bowl of yellow chrysanthemums. I didn't have the impression that Cathy was the one in the house who smoked. Cathy had died about a month before this meditation of brain cancer.

32

I said it was really good to meet her and I am sorry I did not know her in life. I told her that I had been feeling her presence for days. Also, if I was interpreting her words incorrectly, she should try to visualize what she was trying to say to me.

The first thing she said was: "I am sorry I had to leave everyone (she means her family). I want all of you to know that leaving was the most difficult thing I ever had to do. It is hard to be separated to the degree that I am separated from you. I use the word degree because I am (still) very close and will always stay very close."

We then talked about the cancer and her attitude about her inevitable death. She said she had willed herself to die at the end. I found her brimming with energy and mentally very focused. I asked her about the photo and the candle.

I did not know what Cathy's relationship with her stepson had been. I was not sure I was hearing her correctly when she addressed her stepson through me and said: "Did you like that trick? I thought it was pretty good. I know I promised I wouldn't haunt you, but I just had to get your attention." I then saw they had a playful and humorous aspect to their relationship. She continued: "I don't know whether you appreciated my humor (in life) but that was the way I enjoyed relating to you. And of course I did it with huge affection. The teasing was my way of expressing affection for you. I always thought it would be fun to haunt someone (after I died) though. I am not trying to bother you or to purposely upset you."

"I am having the last laugh. I'm having the last word." We both started laughing. She thought moving

33

the photos and the candle was pretty funny. She continued, "It is sort of like saying, I told you so, and there is no way you can answer me. There is nothing you can do back. I am getting the last word, the last joke and last punch line. And that was what that was all about."

Cathy had much more to say which I passed on to family members. This prank she played on her stepson is an illustration of how her playful and loving personality was not changed by death.

When we think about the consistent aspects of our personality through life, we can also, and perhaps inadvertently, be preparing for our death. We get a feeling for our personality while taking a more general view of our choices throughout our life. Our personality is revealed by the characteristics that guided our decisions, our choices.

Choices are the way we exercise our personality. No matter if the choice is good, bad, or indifferent, a choice is always an act of will. Even the choice not to act reflects the will of the personality. When we make choices what criteria do we constantly apply? What values do we hold that make these choices unique to us? What fear or powerlessness are we expressing with our choices? If we think about the consistent attitudes we use to make choices, we may begin to understand our personality.

The way friends or family see us does not necessarily define our personality. Nor is our personality reflected by the children we have devoted so much of our life to. Our children are on their own path. Reviewing life, thinking about the common themes of our choices in

34

life will bring us, to some degree, an understanding of our personality. Honest and introspective evaluation of our traits, our strengths and forgiving ourselves for our weaknesses, will lead to knowledge of our personality.

The overview of a personality can be seen in autobiographies. When we read an autobiography or watch one on TV, we will see a similarity in the attitudes and beliefs a person applied throughout their life. The personality of the author is revealed by what he or she picked from their life events to write about. It is the same when we read or watch a biography.

Few of us take the time to review our choices and think about our personality as we go along in life. Most people review their life in old age or when in the throes of a terminal illness. My maternal grandmother kept every card and letter she was ever sent. In the last few years of her life she would go through them over and over. I believe she was doing the work of achieving self realization before she died. Time spent with photo albums or diaries can be useful tools for developing a sense of our personality. Often the elderly and the dying want to talk about life memories with a care giver. This can also be the work of self realization helping those approaching dying reach a sense of their personality in life.

Many deceased tell me their life flashed before their eyes at the moment of death or just prior to it. This was especially important to those who died unexpected deaths. Life review takes place in an instant in the case of an accidental death. It is necessary to have that sense of the self, the personality, in order to focus and carry that selfhood through the death transition. Understanding the continuity of our personality is a valuable preparation for death, even if it takes place in an instant.

Some years ago a dear friend, Mara, was visiting my home. She was upset because her grandmother was in a coma in a hospital far away, and she had not gotten to say her good-byes. She wanted me to facilitate a conversation with her grandmother. I felt this would not be possible but her distress overruled my skepticism and I decided to try, to do what I could.

I suggested we pray for her grandmother hoping this would build an energy bridge between the two of them. As soon as our intent was voiced in prayer her grandmother was there, out of her body, right in the same room with us. I was able to see and hear her grandmother clearly. I had been so certain this could not happen that I didn't bring a tape recorder into the room with us. You can imagine how much Mara and I regretted that.

I then facilitated a long conversation between Mara and her grandmother. One thing her grandmother said has always stayed with me. She said, approaching death is like packing up your life in cardboard boxes, taping them shut, and knowing nobody will ever open those boxes again. What a way to describe the review of one's life!

Mara called me a few months later to say she had put a rocking chair near the wood stove in her kitchen and laid a crocheted blanket her grandmother had made over the back of the chair. Her grandmother died a few weeks after Mara's visit with me, never physically regaining consciousness. Mara said she often sensed her grandmother sitting in that chair both before and after she died.

I was surprised Mara's grandmother was able to be with us, out of body, before her physical death. Mara's grandmother was also teaching us an important possibility for someone approaching death. When we reach the understanding in life that we are body, mind and spirit or soul, we can believe we continue after death as mind and spirit. But how does this feel? Do we get to practice, take flying lessons before we go? Mara's grandmother did. I was a witness to this possibility again over a decade later.

My husband and I stayed in his parent's home during the last two weeks of his father's life. My husband's father, Sam, was dying of cancer. Sam's ardent wish was to die at home and this was made possible with the support of our local hospice.

I have to digress here and speak to the incredible work that the hospice nurses do. Sam was on morphine but not an adequate amount to ease his pain. His doctor did not want to increase the dose worrying that Sam might become addicted to morphine! My husband's mother did not want him to have more morphine because it agitated Sam. Our hospice nurse knew another drug that, when combined with the morphine, decreased the disorientation and agitation. Hospice made it possible to manage both his pain and his agitation. Sam's suffering would not have been bearable without the intervention of the hospice nurses.

My husband was not concerned about his father's mental rambling, drug induced or not. Once Sam said,

"Let go of my mitten." My husband understood he was holding his father's hand perhaps a little too tightly.

One day Sam seemed to be talking to a person who was already deceased, a person once known as Chicken George. He asked to be taken from his bedroom into the living room because George had come to visit. We got him into the living room to show him George wasn't there. Sam had purchased the land the house was on from George; it was part of the chicken farm George once owned. Sam had known George until George's death. I believe it is entirely possible for the dying to sense other deceased around them. After all, I communicate with the deceased and I do not take morphine.

On another occasion Sam was talking about a man named Jake. Sam described himself in the Civil War and he was badly wounded. He was begging Jake to shoot him and put him out of his misery. My husband did not try to argue his father out of this notion. Perhaps Sam had read this in a book and the story stayed with him. Perhaps it was a past life when someone named Jake really did release him from his pain.

For days Sam had been begging my husband to shoot him. Each time my husband would explain that this would be illegal. Sam finally gave up on my husband as a source for his relief saying, "You didn't help me one bit." These are tough words to hear from a father no matter what the circumstances.

As Sam's death drew closer, I realized what a gift we were being given to be with him as he approached his death. My husband had always been close to his father.

This time was so critical for him to begin to grieve and contemplate life without his father. About ten days before he died Sam said to my husband, "I don't know what is going to happen to me when I die, but I think you do." My husband replied, "yes I do Dad, and you are going to be all right." My husband's lack of fear for his father's transition was conveyed.

A few days before Sam died, he told my husband that he saw a path. My husband asked where the path led and Sam said to a door. But he couldn't get the door open no matter how hard he tried. I believe that was when Sam started to journey out of his body, or at least started to remember doing it.

A few nights later my husband said he thought that his father was standing next to the couch where he was sleeping. When he got up to help Sam back to bed he realized that his father's body was still in the bed. Sam had gone out of body and my husband was sensitive enough to see him. The next night he heard his father call, got up and met his father in the hallway. It seemed as if there was a light behind his Dad, but the hallway light was not on. They didn't speak, but just looked at each other for a long moment. My husband does not remember returning to the couch. I believe they were both out of body together. In spite of these experiences it was heartbreaking to watch Sam's struggle to die.

Sam lapsed into a coma and died a day later. Neither my husband nor I had any doubt he had finally made it through the door at the end of the path. I spoke with Sam, in meditation, a few months after he died. We will hear Sam's perception of these events that occurred as he approached his death in a later chapter.

From Sam and Mara's grandmother we see the dying can practice being out of their body in dream state, or when in a coma. Mara's grandmother and Sam gained a sense of themselves beyond the confines and limitations of their physical body before they died. They explored death, and almost rehearsed the reality of death, so it was familiar to them. I have no doubt this willingness to explore was connected in some degree to their lack of fear of death.

While out of body experiences are a way to prepare for our reality after death, for most of us these will take place, naturally, when we are dreaming. When I change my mental focus in order to meet with the deceased my feelings and mental perceptions are similar to how the deceased feel and perceive. I wouldn't advocate the conscious pursuit of out of body experiences as a preparation for death without the guidance of a trusted and enlightened teacher.

Sometimes doctors will give a patient an idea of how long they have left to live. Friends and family may experience anticipatory grief. In addition, the patient will also begin to grieve their life and prepare for death. This gives everyone a chance to say goodbyes and put things in order. As physical activity becomes more difficult for the dying, their avenue for self expression inevitably becomes more mental and spiritual.

At this point the dying may have a spiritual renewal. If they practiced religion, they may spend more time with their bible or religious publications. My mother certainly did. She had always been a religious person but in the last years of her life she spent much of her time in prayer. Toward the end of her life she seemed to glow golden with her love of God. The dying may also seem to become more childlike because we were all more naturally spiritual as children.

Sometimes, just the pleasure of a warm breeze coming in a window, a bird's song or the beauty of a sunset can evoke feelings of awe and reverence. The kindness of a care giver may also support the dying person's spiritual renewal. A visit from the clergy or a fellow church member can strengthen the thoughts of or awareness of God/Source, reinforcing a spiritual orientation.

At times the change in the personality of the dying is unnerving. Some withdraw from the world as a preparation for death. Some become brutally honest. Some of the dying express emotion we never saw when they were younger. In light of these processes we can offer patience and gentleness. We can communicate acceptance of their transition. We can help them be less fearful by simply providing companionship as they approach their death transition.

We can allow the dying their mental rambling. We may not understand what they are saying, but we should not argue either. The mental wanderings of the elderly may not seem remotely connected to forming the self realization they will need to focus themselves through the death transition. But it is not for us to judge someone else's experience.

An overdose of prescription drugs may inhibit self awareness in the elderly and the dying. Certainly pain management has to be more than adequately addressed. But sometimes tranquillizing drugs, muscle relaxants and sleeping pills are given for the convenience of the care givers, not to benefit the dying. Overuse of these drugs may make it more difficult for the dying to have self awareness as they approach their death transition.

When the elderly and dying are beyond the point of conscious communication, we cannot know where they are in their approach to death. They may be exploring out of body states or they may just be resting, not ready for their journey. We need to give them all the time and comfort we can even if we don't understand their experience.

This brings us to the discussion of euthanasia or suicide by the terminally ill. Euthanasia is the facilitating of a painless death transition. Most of us agree that euthanasia for a suffering pet is a gift of love we give the animal. Some terminally ill people declare their intent to die. If able, they physically participate in the actions that cause their own death or are assisted by a trusted friend or family member. I have meditated with several deceased who enacted self euthanasia without coercion because of a terminal illness. They had conscious transitions and function well in their afterlife.

However, if the decision to die is not made and ideally partially enacted by the dying individual, the dying may be disoriented in their transition and after death reality for a little while. Even though they will eventually achieve self realization and take up the activity in the afterlife, we must never force or coerce a conscious person out of their body against their will. Having said that I would not want to be kept tethered to my body for years or even decades if I was in a vegetative state.

I have communicated with Alzthimers victims and mentally ill people after they have died. Their mental and emotional capacity returns immediately after a death from natural causes. Most said they were not suffering as much while they were alive as it seemed from the perspective of their care givers. I can't know if they would have struggled reaching consciousness had they been forced out of physical. Everyone has the right to reach the end of their learning path on this earth.

We can never judge or condemn a terminally ill and/or elderly person for seeking assisted suicide or committing suicide. The deceased person is the only one that can evaluate if the choice they made was beneficial once they are out of their physical body. So I cannot say that suicide is always wrong. I do think it is important to honor a death and support the family no matter what the circumstances of death.

I call a phenomena related to this a self willed death. It is possible for people to completely leave their body shortly before their physical death. I've been told this by murder victims, and by a few victims of accidental deaths such as drowning or burning. I have worked with deceased who did not feel the majority of the injuries that caused their death. They had already left their body knowing their death was inevitable.

By self-willed death I do not, technically, mean suicide. A self-willed death is a mental and spiritual act of will power. Only the will of the personality is used in a self-willed death to sever the connection with the physical body while with a self euthanasia or suicide some element of physical force is used. A self-willed death is a positive, empowered act. It is the act of willfully embracing and energizing the death transition.

We all have heard of cases with elderly couples where one dies and then the remaining spouse dies of natural causes, or of no discernable cause at all within a matter of days. The spouse who followed certainly enacted a self-willed death.

I recently read an obituary for a local writer who went to the doctors a week before he died because he was not feeling well. He learned he was riddled with cancer and was terminal with or without treatment. His cause of death was listed as a heart attack. It is quite possible this was a self-willed death. One deceased woman I spoke with said she suffered a heart attack in a small hospital and was being transported to another hospital for treatment. She told me she willed herself to die in route. She did not wish to receive treatment or linger as an invalid in a hospital. I read that the elderly Aborigines in Australia could shut down their body's function willfully and die within a half an hour.

A self willed death can be a choice by people who are consciously prepared to die. No matter what causes the death to be an immediate possibility or potential, these people have achieved a degree of self realization. They have a diminished fear of death probably based in the belief they will continue to exist in the afterlife.

I know of a woman who had her daughter make her pre-arrangements with the funeral home as she was dying. Once that was done and she had written her own obituary, she told her daughter the only thing she had left to do now was to pick a date. The mother picked one within a week of that conversation. She died on her chosen date.

A neighbor once told me her dying grandmother had been unconscious for weeks. One day her grandmother woke up, cheerfully said, "Well, here I go," and died. It must take tremendous will power to drop or leave the physical body, severing all ties to it with no culminating physical cause. The mental focus of this choice, no doubt, energizes and sustains the personality through the death transition.

I admire these people. When we are unafraid of the death transition, when we understand our personality will continue as mind and spirit, it is possible to make physical death our life's final creative act.

Chapter Four

Crossing Over

The first thing that happens
when we die is what we believe
will happen to us when we die.

The longer I work with the deceased the more convinced I am that circumstances, experiences and perspectives exist than I ever could learn about in a lifetime. Each deceased person who remembers crossing over tells me their unique story.

I have spoken with many deceased who were conscious or "awake" throughout the death transition. Many of the deceased who had a conscious death, had not been afraid. Before they died, most understood their personality, or at least their soul, would continue in some way or place. I have also worked with many deceased who were not conscious and who could not remember their death transition for various reasons.

Many of the deceased I spoke with, who were conscious during the death process, remembered visualizations they had as they were dying. As the personality, or the mind and spirit of an individual, becomes irrevocably separated from the physical body there is often a visualization+ the dying focus on. I call this a visualization because the dying individual does not see this scene with their eyes. They are comprehending a vision in their mind. Their mind created this vision.

The visualization of an alleyway, a pathway, a road in a column of arching trees or a boat in which to cross a river, are commonly used when crossing out of the body. I call these focusing visualizations. Focusing visualizations can take any form an individual dying person can imagine.

The deceased tell me it can be a challenge to stay focused while the personality is separated from the body and the energies that bind the two are severed. No one I have spoken with said there is pain that accompanies this final phase of death. The pain is over. While this change takes place most deceased say they do sense they are in motion. The death transition is a movement of sorts, but it is a relocation in energy rather than a change of locale.

I think of the physical earth as one plane or level. The near-earth deceased experience is parallel to life but consists of non physical, or a less dense energy. The thin layer of transition energy between these two levels has traditionally been called a veil. When we die or cross over we are crossing through this thin barrier of energy, this veil, that conceals those on the other side from our ordinary senses.

The pathway visualizations serve to hold self awareness within the feeling of movement as the personality passes through the veil and is separated from the physical body. In Sam's case he understood the visualization of a pathway and a door to be his crossing over, or crossing out of physical life. The road or pathway seems real to the dying, and it is as real as anything else projected by their mind. The focusing visualization is simply a tool the mind uses when leaving the physical body.

Some deceased tell me they didn't remember having a focusing visualization when they died. Perhaps they just didn't need it. Whenever I go through one of those drive through car washes I feel like this would be a good visualization to use when I die. I've always felt a bit nervous in those machines and keep my eyes glued on the daylight coming through the exit doors.

Most people, when they die, will also see or be aware of previously deceased people who greet them. Sometimes these greeters are still near the earth. They have purposefully remained near their loved ones to be as close as they can. They are already in the immediate location of a beloved dying individual. All these greeters, as I call them, are from the other side of the thin veil of death transition energy. It is perfectly understandable then that the dying perceive the greeters or predeceased friends or family as being at the other end of the pathway, tunnel, roadway or across the river.

Ancestors that are our greeters can also come to meet the dying from further away, from higher or more energized levels of the afterlife. These greeters may appear surrounded by bright light because they embody greater personal energy.

The disincarnate or pre-deceased people who greet us after death serve two incredibly important functions for the dying. It is easier to leave our body behind if we have something to move toward. Our attention is then drawn away from our physical body to someone else. The love of the pre-deceased people present at our death also represents something warm, inviting, perhaps safe and bright.

Most of the deceased I spoke with who crossed over with ease were moving toward ancestors, predeceased parents or spouses, or their deceased children. The predeceased relatives are not just a figment of a dying person's imagination. Our deceased loved ones greet us by choice and with purpose. These disincarnate people who greet us are the midwives of our death.

51

One young deceased girl I spoke with said she was staying the age that her mother last saw her so when she greeted her mother she would look the same. This girl died when she was 16 and has already served as her grandfather's greeter. It is both an honor and a pleasure for the deceased to fulfill this role for their loved ones.

We can also be greeted by the God we were devoted to in life. Christ the Savior might greet those who loved him. The Blessed Mother may be there for those devoted to her. Christ, the Blessed Mother, the saint we were devoted to, Buddha, Vishnu, Baha'u'llah or Mohammed do not take away our free will, they do not take over and make our choices for us. The deceased who are greeted by God, know God is their ultimate destination. Our religious relationship with God continues in the afterlife much the same as it was in life. Some deceased have no religious affiliation or no belief in a personification of God. Often, for these deceased, if a light or brightness is perceived at the other end of their focusing visualization it represents God/Source, love or unity.

The second function of the greeters is to teach us. Predeceased loved ones can explain to the newly deceased that they are out of their body, but have survived their death. A deceased person who does not believe they will exist beyond death can be helped tremendously by the predeceased. They can achieve self realization, while without help they may have floundered for a short period. Love is the key to this help. People may have plenty of predeceased relatives but if there was no love between them in life there may be no abiding attachment in the afterlife either.

The greeters also explain to the dying that they can remain near the earth. From the greeters we learn what we can, heal what we can, and then take up our afterlife as individually as we did in life.

A variety of spiritually evolved beings other than the deceased's relatives can also greet the dying. I see this particularly in the death of children where they may not have a close attachment to anyone who has predeceased them. Small children may not have formed an understanding of God/Source as a persona. Often, there is no one that dying children would be eager enough to see to turn away from their parents. But whether it is Grandma or Gabriel who leads them, children are ushered with particular care and love into the afterlife. Without exception, all children have helpers.

This help offered by the greeters seems to only happen at the moment of death. Some deceased who were not conscious when they died tell me that they did not remember having this type of help later when they were "awake". It is possible they consciously missed this initiation while dying. It is also possible for the deceased to ask for and receive help, in various ways from any number of disincarnate individuals, and at any point in the afterlife.

I did a reading with a client in the Midwest whose mother had died, then a year or so later I meditated again with her and her now deceased father. As a couple, her parents were greeting and helping other elderly people who died without a belief they would survive their death.

But it was not all work for this deceased couple, they also went dancing and attended a lot of concerts together. They were still a social, loving outgoing couple and it was my pleasure to meet them both.

As the dying concentrate on the focusing visualization and the messages from those who greet them, the bond with their physical body is severed. We can think of this like a thread that links us to our body in the same way the umbilical chord attaches us to our mother at birth. The thread of energy connecting our personality to our physical body may break easily in the death transition, when we are distracted by a visualization or by greeters.

I believe the people who have Near Death Experiences left their body and had a focusing visualization often described as a tunnel. Some have conversations to report that they had with guides or deceased relatives. People who had a Near Death Experience say they have less fear about their death after this event than they did before it. However, the energy thread connecting their personality to their body was perhaps stretched but was not severed. They did not die. Many people who remembered having a Near Death Experience were conscious while they left their body and may or may not have been conscious as they returned to their body.

As a medium, I sometimes work for living clients who are not at peace with the way their loved one died. A percentage of my work, then, is with deceased who may still be struggling to achieve self realization after death. I wouldn't say a conscious death is better. There is no correct way to die. But I find the more conscious the dying and the newly deceased are, the greater their ease at adapting to and finding meaningful activity in their afterlife.

We still have free will after we die and there are so many reasons why the dying may not be conscious during their death transition. We will look at more of the reasons self realization is harder for some deceased in later chapters. I want to address beliefs here, however, because the first thing we experience as we are dying is what we believe will happen when we die. Strong or adamant beliefs about death can limit or prevent consciousness during and for a while after the death transition.

How we believe our death will "feel" or take place is carried in our mind through the death transition. The reason these beliefs are our first experience when dying is because the mental and spiritual, immaterial reality is so new to us. If we believe we will experience a nothingness, a void, the mind will carry that reality into death and construct blackness, a void, or however the belief of nothingness was understood. People who believe they will experience heaven immediately upon death can project that reality in their mind as well. But projected beliefs carried in the mind do not last for several reasons.

The dying person who expects to disappear will experience the blackness, a void of sorts. But eventually they will come to the logical conclusion that if they are experiencing anything at all, even a void, they must still exist. Self preservation remains a human trait in the afterlife. Someone who is suffering after death from a belief in annihilation will eventually seek an end to this suffering. They may wish for or ask for help, and that is all it takes to make a change in their mental reality.

I was assured, by one of my clients, that I would enjoy the meditation with a nurse who had died of cancer. She had been a loving wife, mother and friend to all who crossed her path. I was taken aback when I found her still mentally focused in the hospital where she died. She was still waiting to get well and did not know she was dead. As soon as I got her convinced of her state, she looked at me and said: "what am I doing with you, I want to go to my family!" With that she was gone. We connected again for my client months later. She had died under the influence of morphine, but I have met other deceased people for whom morphine does not cause confusion. I often work for parents and with deceased young people who die of accidental overdoses and have yet to find one not aware of their deceased state.

Being deceased is not a passive state of inactivity. In the personality's impetus toward action, temporary realities created by belief will dissolve. Spending time immersed in a projected belief will delay learning and function in the afterlife, but only as long as it takes to mentally work through these projected beliefs. Some people's projected belief of what their afterlife will be like is based in the religion they practiced in life.

I have no doubt in my mind that a spiritual orientation casts death in a positive light for people who believe in God/Source, unity and love. However, I feel the power so many religions seem to have on people is related to people's fear of death. Some religions promote their own, exclusive heaven, where only members of their church will abide after death. Members of the same religion may well form a group in the human species consciousness pool, as discussed in Chapter 10. That may be the exclusive heaven they anticipate.

Some religions promise purgatory or hell if specific religious rituals are not preformed, no matter how kind and loving a person is in life. It doesn't matter what religion we practice, or even if we practice none at all. People with any degree of self realization, from any race, creed or culture can learn and progress in the afterlife.

I think many individuals can turn away from religion, from spirituality, from the concept of unity and universal love, away from God/Source because the combination of a judgmental and loving God just doesn't make sense. Since this judgment is supposed to happen at the moment of death, no wonder people fear death! If we are afraid of judgment at the moment of death we may not experience death as consciously as if we are fearless. There are no rules after death and our only judgment is self created and self inflicted.

Not one of us hasn't done something we regret in life. Perhaps we tried to make amends. Perhaps amends were not possible. Learning to be a good human by making mistakes is different from a life dedicated to destructive acts and to evil. Sensible, decent people should not be troubled by fear of self judgment within their death transition.

I was asked, once, to work with a young man in Canada who died of an AIDS related illness. In meditation, I found Terry in a hospital cafeteria setting. He was still dressed in his hospital gown and a robe. Terry was fairly introverted and didn't trust me, but I was able to help him somewhat.

Early in our conversation he said he couldn't wait to get out of the hospital. I explained to him he was empowered to discharge himself. He replied that he still felt pain and felt he still needed to be in the hospital. I worked with his belief until I got him to hold the image of himself at an age before his illness, before the pain. Once he had grasped that concept, he had another reason why he couldn't leave the hospital.

He said he had no clothes, and flashed me the image of the clothes he was cremated in. He said, " I can't wear those, they are all burned up." I told him he can mentally dress himself in any outfit he chooses. We had a good laugh because he showed me he had some really wild clothes when he was alive. I suggested comfortable clothing and he put on a baggy cotton sweater and corduroys. At this point, we had changed his age and clothes so I knew we were getting somewhere. I walked him out of the hospital and out onto the grounds a little way. I asked him where he had lived and he said pretty far away. He had come home to die. I asked him if he felt like he could go to his family home but he said he was estranged from his mother. He said there was a sister he felt close to so I suggested he go to her apartment until he understood his new reality more. I explained to him how he could move around to get to her apartment.

I also explained that prayer was a way he could heal and energize himself.

What Terry's story shows is an absolute lack of beliefs about what the afterlife experience would be. He was caught up in rather limited possibilities, even though he remembered being cremated, so he must have known he was dead. He had no thought about what to do, so he stayed in the hospital.

I think Terry would have eventually figured things out without my intervention. After all, he was not up in the room where he had died. He knew that bed was occupied. He also knew he still existed even though his body had been cremated. He did not realize yet that he was creating his own experience. But he would. If Terry had asked for help, or been open to it, there are so many that would have come to his aid from the other side of the veil, I just got to him first.

One thing I still find remarkable as I work with the deceased is they are far less interested in talking about the manner of their death, and what the experience was like, than I am. Terry's actual death never came up in the conversation. He was skeptical of my help so I was just trying to give him all the information I could. It was not the time for me to do research.

I have found most deceased are not concerned with their physical body or what happened to it. The only deceased person I ever communicated with concerned with her physical remains was a murder victim. She was trying to help me find her body in a nearby large river so her murderer could be convicted. She had been deceased for over two years at this point. She said the bag containing what was left of her body was snagged on a root and covered in silt. We organized several diving teams which reported the configuration of the river bottom was as she described it. Sadly, we were not able to find her body.

I was once asked to meditate by the mother of a missing and presumed deceased son. Of course I was overwhelmed by the emotional responsibility, so I asked for help from two young deceased people I had worked with already from the same area. With their help I was able to find my client's son in spirit. The missing man's body has washed down stream after he accidently drown and was completely disintegrated. He was pleased that his body had become part of the natural world that he had loved so much in life.

I make a point of asking every deceased person I talk to what their experience of death was. Most remember their death. Most of the deceased I work with say the manner of their death nor the disposition of their remains is important to them, certainly not as important as these things are to us. Once conscious, the newly deceased are immersed in thinking about their prior life and exploring the possibilities in this new reality.

Chapter Five

The Newly Deceased

Self realization and assimilation are
the first tasks of the newly deceased.

The movie Beetlejuice was about a young couple who died in an automobile accident. They did not like the people who bought their house after they died and tried to drive the new owners out. Right after they died, they were in the attic of their house and they found a book called: Handbook for the Recently Deceased. When we die, wouldn't it be great if there was such a book? Maybe there is, but no deceased person has ever mentioned it to me.

While there is no handbook, the newly deceased do have help, if they are open to it, from people on earth and also from the other side. From the earth comes the love energy transmitted to them when we pray for and remember the deceased. There are also mediums here on earth who do what we can for selected deceased. From the other side, predeceased friends and relatives greet, help heal and inform the newly deceased.

I am also finding that the deceased can form groups and help each other near the earth. Some deceased young people gather with others from their same area. They help each other and sometimes say they just hang out and go to movies together. I've even called on young deceased, who are now my friends, to help with others I become aware of that might need help- a kind of networking among the deceased, so to speak.

The newly deceased are never without help in the afterlife. If they ask for help, help is there. But no one else does the "work" of self realization, assimilation, healing and progression for them.

There can be a sense of floating, of unreality for some newly deceased people when they die. Death is the last tangible memory, so they will mull over that experience first. Gradually they will begin to "look around" and orient themselves to this new reality. Self realization is the process the deceased use to learn to function in the afterlife. Self realization means taking stock of what they consist of, which is mind and spirit. They realize what they have to work with in their here and now, within their present.

Carried in the mind of the deceased is an echo of their physical body. Through the process of self realization the deceased become familiar with the "body" they have when we are newly deceased. The deceased know they are not in their physical body, and yet they still feel as if they are to some extent. They feel the parameters of themselves and the outline is the same shape as they had when in a body. For a large person it will be a large echo, for a baby, a baby's echo.

This echo looks like a three-dimensional slide projection. In fact it is a projection of the deceased's mind. To the deceased, this looks like a holographic image of their body and it seems real and tangible because they are within it. As one deceased person expressed it, "we clothe ourselves with the memory of the prior body at whatever age is desired."

I used to describe this holographic projection in a three-word phrase, the sensory memory body. That was because this energy body seems to be interpreting information in a similar way the nervous system was when they were in a physical body. The deceased sense things, but these senses are based on the memory of sensual experience. Thus, memory was the second word of my phrase. Body is the third word because this holographic projection is the vehicle for the mind, spirit, and personality of the deceased.

I have now stopped using the word sensory. The newly deceased and the deceased near the earth do have a stronger ability to remember sensory experience because they are still within the proximity of the earth. But as they progress in the afterlife the need to feel things as they did on earth dims or recedes. The deceased's own perception of their memory body changes or evolves in the afterlife. We will see how and why in later chapters.

The memory body does not seem to be self generated to the newly deceased. It is not even important for the newly deceased to realize their body is a projection of their mind. They will simply utilize the memory body as they learn about their new reality.

We saw in the last chapter how Terry eliminated the memory of, or the belief, that he was in pain in his afterlife experience by mentally changing his age to a time before his illness. This is something most deceased figure out quickly. This is an important first learning step for the newly deceased as they begin to create their own reality in the afterlife.

For some deceased, changing the idea of their memory body is absolutely necessary to their function in the afterlife. This is particularly important when the physical body was dismembered or disfigured at death. When the memory of the disfigurement is projected by the mind of the deceased, they have to mentally change their memory body so that they can feel whole again. I worked with a young burn victim several times during the first year after she died. It was incredibly difficult for her to not think about the level of pain she died in and the trauma to her body. Eventually she did heal sufficiently to envision her body prior to her accident.

Often when I work with the deceased, I perceive their memory body at a very different age than they were when they died. I will see them in what the deceased consider the prime of their life. This changing of self perception to a healthy age or to a whole body is actually the first of the healing activities the deceased may accomplish. If there was a handbook for the recently deceased this "turning back the clock" would be in the first chapter.

I remember working for a friend with his deceased mother. He was concerned for his mother's welfare in the afterlife because as she died she said to her son, "I'll never be happy again." This haunted my friend because his mother had been such an optimist in life. After the meditation, I described the woman the way she appeared to me, complete with hair style and dress. He was convinced this was not his mother because of the way I described her. Many months later he called me. He found an old photograph of his mother taken in the nineteen thirties in the exact dress and hair style I described. Finally he believed the message his mother had given me to pass on to him. She wanted him to know that she had been afraid as she was dying that she would never be happy again, but was indeed happy in her afterlife.

When the deceased can change their "age" in order to feel healed and vigorous again they have made a choice based on the assimilation of knowledge about their memory body. Another choice self realization makes possible is that of movement. Movement for the deceased is simply a matter of concentration and will. When they focus their mind on a destination, they will find themselves there.

Many deceased discover movement almost by accident. Remember Charlene from the first chapter? In trying to find her partner she thought she had to walk home from the hospital. Then she found herself moving really fast and that was frightening to her. She had not gotten used to zooming around yet. Other deceased follow roads to relocate, imagining they are going at the same speed as they did in cars. Some learn to move by simply following the people they love at whatever pace the living are going.

Many newly and conscious deceased first discover how to move when they follow the earthly remains of their body as it is moved. Many stay with their body as it is transported from the hospital to the funeral home, and on to the crematory or graveyard. We can be quite sure that the conscious deceased are there, attending their funeral, out of body.

Assimilation is also a task for the newly deceased. The definition of assimilation is translating experience into knowledge. Assimilation is a big word for thinking things over or figuring things out. There is a lot to figure out about the afterlife. Often the first thing we think about is how we died. If we remember how this transfer in energy took place, we can work at becoming objective about the experience. We understand that it is in the past, something that happened to us, but something that does not take our attention from the present reality.

Getting beyond the experience of death is harder in the case of traumatic deaths. What is interesting is that I have spoken to people who died in their sleep and the experience was traumatic for them. I have also spoken to people whose body was mangled in auto accidents who did not consider their deaths traumatic.

I find traumatic deaths most often in people whose death prevented them from fulfilling their life mission, work or intent. An example is parents separated from their living children by death. This tragic element has an emotional impact on the deceased and adds to the work of assimilating, or coming to be at peace with their death. Some deceased must grieve their death before they can do anything else. I have worked with deceased entrenched in denial and anger. The personal trauma of death then has to be processed mentally and emotionally, much the same way a trauma would need to be resolved in life.

What caused their death and how it took place can be reviewed in the mind of the deceased until the emotional impact wears off. The deceased may have to substitute positive or distracting thoughts about the manner of their death until some of its emotional impact fades. Assimilation of the manner of death is complete when the way they died is not their focus anymore. It is a bit like when we finally get past our childhood issues or traumas and don't think about them anymore.

The deceased can then think things over and assimilate their surroundings. Their mind is no different from what it was in life, consisting of the same intellect and memory. Intellect includes reasoning ability and creativity. Memory is the understanding of events in sequential order. Memory includes past emotional and sensual experience. Memories of the prior life are patterns that have stayed in the deceased's mind. The deceased also add to their memory the events that have transpired since their death.

Emotion is also possible for the newly deceased. Since they do not have the endocrine system that they had in the physical body, emotion is a function of memory as well. Emotion, however, fades quickly for most of the deceased I have worked with. At times when I am meditating, I will be crying at the beauty or the sadness of their story and they will, by contrast, be relatively dispassionate and objective.

I think the desire to remember negative emotion fades quickly in most deceased because negative emotions are not helpful and are not a productive use of their mental energy. As one young woman put it, they can no longer think unproductive thoughts, and when they do she takes, what she calls her golden eraser, and erases the negative thought symbolically from her mind. And believe me, when these young people see their family struggling to simply survive, it can cause great pain in the deceased. Through will power and self discipline, the deceased choose to cultivate, sustain, and practice positive emotion much as they did in life.

The deceased have the same mental outlook on their spirituality as they did in life. The mind of the deceased incorporates the empowerment of the soul or spirit. The soul is the receptor for the unlimited God/Source energy that we draw into ourselves through prayer. I have a friend who considers his soul his internal compass. No matter what he is doing in life, his soul is always oriented toward God/Source. The deceased have, to the extent they are aware of it, this interceptor of God's love and this internal compass which will guide them home to God/Source.

Self realization and the assimilation of experience results in knowledge. Knowledge results in possibilities, and choices within the new possibilities. Assimilation happens at different rates for everyone. Lack of fear makes assimilation easier. But we don't score any points for how fast we can change our age or move around after we die. Just to learn what is possible is the important thing for the newly deceased. Many deceased become familiar with their memory body, change their age and move around in a split second. Others take things slowly, one step at a time as they begin to learn that they direct their reality in the afterlife.

I visited Sam, my father-in-law, who we met in the previous chapter, shortly after he died. In meditation I had the image of the back yard of his house. In the meditation it was summer and we (mentally) got two aluminum lawn chairs out of the shed to sit on while we talked. At first there were such undercurrents of emotion that we just held hands and prayed for a minute or so.

He had already changed his age to just before the cancer had caused his physical decline. He was wearing the flannel shirt, chinos and moccasins his family had so thoughtfully chosen to bury him in. As I tossed white light toward him to test his image, we laughed because the container was an old-fashioned milk pail. His image then became much more distinct.

I asked Sam if he would share with me how he experienced his death. He said, "Death felt natural for me. I just got out of bed, walked down the hall and sat in my chair in the living room. All in all, life is continuing pretty much the same for me. I decide if I am going shopping with my (still living) wife, or whether to just hang around the house. I also keep tabs on what is going on in town."

"I remember my son was trying to help me learn about being out of my body when he was dreaming. Part of me didn't believe it. Part of me thought those were just hallucinations. I remember being out of my body and my son coming down the hall toward me. I assumed that the light over my shoulder was my guardian angel. It wasn't as if I believed it even though I was doing it."

"I don't understand why sometimes I could go out of my body during those last days and other times I couldn't, I would try to get out, will myself to die. I don't understand why I did not have any control over that.

"I didn't feel like I had much control over events in my life either, only over myself and how I chose to be. I wanted a peaceful life and took small steps at a time. It wasn't so much safety. I wanted things in scale. So many things did not have attraction for me, things didn't

71

interest me. It wasn't as if I had wanted to be an explorer and lived with a burning desire to go to remote places and was unfulfilled. After the war (WW II) I just wanted peace and calm in my life. There were many things I didn't want that were part of my life. Some of those things are inevitable. You can't pick your relatives." (We laugh)

"I wanted to keep my life on a manageable scale. I am still doing that. I see no point in exploring now. I am content to follow the rhythm of my wife's days. I really thought things over in life as I went along. I can't say it is much different for me now."

We continued visiting for a little while. I asked if I might come again sometime, before I thanked him and ended the meditation. In fact I have not visited Sam again in meditation, because he has remained a loved and loving presence in our lives. My husband knows they are together at times in dream state, and sometimes when he is on the tractor or cutting wood he feels his Dad close by.

When we are young, we think our reality is determined by others. We tend to define our self through our family's opinions, our schoolmates, friends or the media. As we age, we cease to hang our identity on events or other people's attitudes about us. We get tired of the ups and downs we go through when people change their opinions of us, or when events outside our control make us feel lucky or unlucky. We gradually learn that our sense of self can only come from within.

When people's praise or criticism of us has less meaning for us, we know we are becoming more centered in our own perception of our reality. When we have an unchanging sense of ourselves no matter what is going on around us, we can begin to understand that we really do create our life. This knowledge will serve us well in life and in the afterlife.

This was one of the most important things I learned from the deceased that I applied to my life. The deceased can no longer depend on what is outside of them to determine their reality. In life we have the pressure of jobs, housework, schedules and it is easy to believe that what is outside of us dictates reality. While in fact it is only our subjective consideration of the job and schedule that determines our reality. If you remove all the immediate props of physical life, which is what happens at death, it becomes evident immediately how we create our own reality by how we think and what we believe to be true.

The newly deceased consider the advice of the predeceased greeters who come to guide and teach them. But the deceased have to learn to direct their own experience in the afterlife. Without the props of the material world and without the necessary tasks we had in life there are no other options but to create reality within the mind. Being deceased is a completely self directed mental and spiritual reality. This is not a difficult or a negative thing. It's just really different at first.

If the newly deceased don't know something is possible for them then they can't choose that possibility. Assimilation of our afterlife experience, the reality we are immersed in, is the way we explore those possibilities. There are as many possibilities as there are deceased people because everyone is different. The more you know you can do in the afterlife, the more you can experience.

I want to share another story of a newly deceased man named Bert. He had evolved to the point that he was at least willing to explore his choices. I'll let Bert tell you his experiences in his own words.

"When I died, I rose slowly and easily to the ceiling over my bed. I could see all the people in the room. I didn't think about what I was doing. I just stayed close to my family. I did look toward the light when I died and part of my mind did move toward it. It was the light that told me I could stay with my wife. There were a lot of people on the other side. They wanted me to know I was dead but I could stay where I was."

"I stayed with my body as it was wheeled out of the house, and later when it was at the funeral home. I wanted to see who came to visit me (during calling hours). I was right there with my wife for all of that. That is how she got through it so well, she knew I wasn't gone."

"When my wife was alive, she talked to me and I talked to her. That is why she never cried as much as people expected her to. I was in between, not living but not feeling dead either. But when my wife died (about six years later) I felt like I died then too. It was like I hadn't been dead until she died. She was my anchor until then. She moved past me quickly and I was thrown into utter panic and confusion. I was distraught about her death because I thought we would be together."

"That is where you found me the first time you came. I was in a crowd and I was lost and I didn't know what to do. You helped me create this room to be in where I could be alone and think things over. I'm not worried about being here (in the room that is Bert's own thought construction). I know I am in my present. I am aware of the things that happen to those I love on earth. I don't feel like doing much more than just thinking about my life. I feel like things are going to get better for me but I have to open those doors for myself. "

I see many couples together in the afterlife and I see many who are not. It was Bert's choice to remain near his wife while she was on earth. It was her choice to move on when she died. I cannot judge either choice.

Sam and Bert's stories emphasize that the essential nature of the deceased does not change simply because they do not have a physical body. When I contact a person who was not outgoing in life they are not going to be very gregarious in their communication with me. With shy people, I find that my first contact can be more of an introductory experience for them. If we have a second conversation or meditation, they may be more communicative.

When I do psychic work for living clients I advise them not expect their deceased loved one to now be able to pick the winning lottery numbers. Probably their deceased loved one won't be able to tell them how to fix all their problems either. If the deceased couldn't do these things in life how could they be expected to do those things after death?

What the deceased can do is show or tell me enough details, in ways specific to them, to provide some solace for their grieving families. But we can't expect a person who dies when they are nineteen to have the mental and emotional scope of a person who died after a long and full life. People simply don't change that much immediately after death.

The newly deceased have to begin experience where they were emotionally, mentally and spiritually when they died. Sometimes the newly deceased may have a healing experience first, before they can do anything else. One woman I spoke to left her body when it was removed from the house, went to her welcoming ancestors, and was never concerned with her discarded physical body again. She was not present at, or aware of, her cremation. After a degree of healing was achieved with her ancestors, her focus did return to the earth well before her memorial service.

Through self realization and assimilation of their current condition the newly deceased will de-construct the beliefs that cloud their initial reality and limit their choices. They learn what is possible in their memory body. They learn they have choices within what they understand is possible. At first they may grieve the loss of their physical life, they may be angry or feel tremendous guilt. As the newly deceased work through these emotions and gain more knowledge, things in the afterlife will get better for them. But in order to get their "sea legs" most stay near the earth, at least for a while.

Chapter Six

Near-Earth Deceased

The deceased do not feel they have
lost the living,
it is the living that feel they have lost
the deceased.

My ability to mentally be with the deceased is a responsibility. I have the responsibility to help who I can and to pass along what I know to you. My ability to mentally be with the deceased is also a gift. I feel gifted, especially when I can meet and speak with women such as Beryl Markham. My meditation with Beryl ends this chapter. Her story illustrates so much that is possible when we are deceased and still near the earth.

We can stay near the earth for as long as we wish after we die. We will have no reason to leave the people, places and things that we loved in life. We can more easily reach self awareness, heal from the manner of our death and assimilate our experience near comforting reference points.

For some deceased, remaining where they died or were buried is not a deliberate choice. That is simply where they find themselves. They stay there until they learn to move around. Other deceased, attached to the idea of their physical body, may stay at the cemetery or mausoleum because they are unwilling to leave their body. The deceased may linger near their home as an orientation point because they can't think of anywhere else they would rather be.

I worked with one young man who died in a boating accident and stayed near the remains of his physical body for several months. It was as if he was sitting a prolonged shiva for himself. His body was never found by the living, it had washed down into a swamp area. Then winter came and his remains were iced over, eventually they dissolved. Oddly, he was pleased that his body became part of nature, which he had loved so much in physical.

A few deceased who have tragic deaths feel the need to stay near the actual site of their death. Sometimes these people are not conscious enough, after they die, to have seen their body taken away or follow it through their wake, funeral and their body's disposition. It may take them a while to remember the instant before they died, and figure out how they got to be where they are now. If they died in unfamiliar surroundings, they may not know, for a while, that they can go home or how to move to get there. Some healing and assimilation will have to take place before these near-earth deceased can begin to make choices. Again, help is readily available and all they have to do is ask for it and it is given by their own guides, ancestors or other deceased dedicated to this work.

There are also deceased who stay near the earth although they know there are higher levels of energy they can inhabit. Most deceased hesitate to leave beloved people and places and will mingle with the earth reality, as much as possible, for a period.

Some deceased stay near the earth to enjoy nature's beauty even though their experience of nature is modified. Our enjoyment of nature will not be as acute as it was when we were in a body. It will be based on the memory of physical sensation. The deceased's experience will be the memory of what this would have looked like and felt like when they were in a body. The deceased's ability to experience joy in the natural world is dependent on how much they appreciated the natural world when they were alive.

Another reason deceased people stay near the earth is that they have unfinished business here. A deceased individual will take the opportunity to stay near a person, animal, place or event where there is something left unresolved. This relationship may be one of love or it can be rooted in a lingering conflict. The deceased work toward a satisfactory conclusion to relationships even if this resolution can only happen within their own mind.

I am quite sure that some of my readings are instigated by the deceased themselves. My guess is that when a deceased is aware of a medium near their loved one they may urge them to seek one out. Unfinished business, such as the location of a will or other important papers, is sometimes the catalyst. I don't know how many of my clients are led to me by their deceased loved ones, but I suspect it is more than a few.

Another interesting possibility exists for the near-earth deceased. I read years ago that the deceased who die young can continue to age as if they were still alive. I personally encountered this with a young deceased family member who had decided to live by our clock. He was organizing his "days" around that of his still living family. He was going to mentally age in his memory body as if he was still in physical (body) along with the rest of his family.

Several times in meditation, I have encountered family members who died together, staying together in the near-earth deceased experience. I often see couples and their pets staying together. But I have not seen a lot of random interaction among unrelated or previously unknown deceased people in the near-earth deceased experience. However there is no reason why the deceased can't or shouldn't form new meaningful friendships with other deceased in the early stages of the afterlife.

In my work I found many deceased choose to have as much, if not more, solitary experiences than social ones, especially in the early stages of the afterlife. Some mediums write that we are guided every step of the way by the predeceased or other spiritual guides. Other mediums write that we are all organized into groups and our activities are planned for us. While I have found that the deceased may voluntarily form groups in any experience level, my research leads me to believe that, ultimately, we learn to navigate the afterlife for ourselves.

Charlene, who we met in the first chapter, and I had a wonderful conversation a few years after her death. One question I asked her was about socializing in the near-earth deceased experience. She said, "I am not socializing much, you don't really need to, you don't feel alone. I still can see the living people on earth and other deceased that I can sense all around me. I might catch someone's (a deceased person's) eye and kind of laugh or point to something and know that we are both seeing the same thing in the same way, but it is not like we become buddy-buddy."

"There is a close friend that will be joining me, and even as dreadful as her illness is, this has given me something to look forward to. Once she gets over losing her body it is not so bad out here. There is lots to think about and in so many ways it is so much easier. Obviously there aren't some of the perks (of being alive) but there is not the hassle."

Charlene was still close to the surface of the earth, going between her home in Pennsylvania and Florida, "visiting" her mother. She said she was having fun standing around in spring (baseball) training. As she said laughing, "The players can't even see you." She also goes to Disney World because "it's free", and added, "You think there are a lot of living people there, believe me, there are tons of dead people there too". She got me really laughing when she said, " I can eat and eat and I don't gain an ounce".

I knew Charlene had been close to horses in life so I asked her if she was doing anything with horses now. She said she walks with a group of horses that are turned out not far from where she lived. "They can see me clearly. I only walk with them at night in the moonlight because I don't want to deal with anyone else." By this she means a living person. I asked her if she ever gets on one of them to ride. She answered, "I am not sure if that would frighten them. I would have no bridle to control them with, not that I can be hurt. But I really don't want to spook them." Charlene and I continued a long conversation with many messages for living friends and family. I'm so happy I can enjoy her optimism, teasing and goofy sense of humor again.

Some near-earth deceased remain near a loved one to act as a guardian. Grandparents or other ancestors often stay near living family to act as guides. My friend

Sarah once asked me to work with her sister, who had recently died. I could not reach her sister who had been mentally disabled for her whole life. The information came that the sister was now integrated in a group, a hive soul, of similar deceased and was not self knowing in an individual way.

Instead, Sarah's deceased mother came with an urgent message for Sarah's daughter, Beth, who was living in England. The grandmother said to tell Beth that when she starts to have stomach pain to not ignore it and to get to the hospital right away. Only a month or so after this meditation Beth's life was saved by her grandmother's message. Beth's appendix burst just after reaching the hospital. I will never know how the grandmother knew this was a possibility for Beth, I was just grateful that Sarah respected my work enough to tell Beth what her grandmother had said.

The deceased perceive us as if they are looking through a one way mirror. We don't see them. We are on the reflective side of the mirror. But unlike a mirror, this barrier is not flat. The deceased are all around us.

In our culture any brush with the deceased is considered to be in the realm of ghosts. But the deceased are not ghosts. An accurate description of ghosts is contained in a later chapter. At times, people call or write me because they have had some sort of interaction with the deceased and they seek to validate or understand that experience. I think many people are sensitive enough to feel when a deceased loved one is nearby. A common experience for the living is to smell pipe smoke or a particular perfume in unlikely places. Yes, these deceased can be nearby and are trying to let us know they still exist.

A deceased person can sometimes communicate when a living friend, relative, or loved one is asleep. While not all the dreams we have about the deceased are communication, there may be some lingering or emotionally charged aspect that makes the dream unforgettable. The dream may evoke a feeling of resolution to the relationship. The living person may feel better or differently about the deceased or experience a softening of the grief.

A friend told me that she had a powerful dream with her grandfather after he died. She was a teenager at the time. She dreamed her grandfather called her on the telephone. She swears she had picked up the phone next to her bed even though she was asleep. She remembers talking to him for a long time. The grandfather wanted her to find a manuscript he had written. She never did find his manuscript but she cherishes this memory.

A number of people tell me stories about their deceased loved ones and telephones. My favorite was a couple who was watching a movie upstairs. They heard the telephone ring downstairs and weren't going to answer it, but they had a pot of spaghetti sauce on the stove to check. On the way downstairs they smelled gas-the burner had blown out and the gas had filled the air downstairs. They turned off the burner, grabbed the phone and the cat and ran outside. After the house was safely aired out they wanted to find out who called to thank them for possibly saving their lives. There was no record of the call on their caller ID. They even *69ed and an earlier call was dialed. They had the distinct feeling their phone call had come from the other side. Someone was watching out for them. After all, telephones are instruments of communication.

One woman told me that after her husband died she was standing on her deck near the ocean and a seagull came and hovered in front of her for several minutes. Her husband had loved watching the gulls. She said she felt his presence while that gull was there. A mother whose son had recently died had a family gathering at her house after the funeral. She said it was pouring rain all around them but her house was in a shaft of sunlight. More than one of her guests commented that this was her son letting them know he was OK. Other people tell me stories of dragonflies or butterflies following them around while they are outside for prolonged periods and feeling that their beloved deceased was somehow instrumental in this occurrence. Wishful thinking, perhaps, but when we are changed by these events it is possible they are communications from the other side.

A magnificent young horse of mine died tragically a few years ago. About a year after she died, I was staying at a friend's farm in New Jersey where this horse had once boarded. Sparkle used to not only break out of her own pasture but she would even let out one or two of the other horses and they would enjoy their freedom, much to the annoyance of the farm owner. On the night I slept there, I heard the sound of hooves pounding outside the house that woke me up. I listened a while longer but didn't hear it again. In the morning I asked if any of the horses that lived there had gotten loose during the night. None had. The change in my grief convinced me that this was Sparkle's way of saying goodbye. Ever since she died, I had a pain in my heart like a knife wound. When I woke up that morning it was gone. And while I still grieve her, these thoughts do not cause the sharp, almost physical pain, that her loss had caused before this happened.

A more tangible form of communication from the near-earth deceased has to do with energy transfer. The energy enhancement of a blooming tree, flower or bush is a fairly common expression of endearment from the deceased. The deceased transfer some of their personal energy to the plant. The more spiritually advanced the deceased had been in life, the more likely that they can accomplish this.

One of my aunts visited some years ago with about two dozen photos of a lilac bush that was next to her home in Alaska. The bush rarely blossomed in all the years it had been there. But the spring after my uncle died it was so overloaded with blossoms it was hard to tell it had leaves. I think my aunt knew who had caused these blossoms although she didn't say that in so many words.

I don't think many people can miss these displays of love by the deceased. But we may just not believe it is possible. It is unfortunate when these kinds of displays of love are overlooked by the living. They are such beautiful gestures of abiding love.

When a dream changes our grief and makes it more bearable we have to allow that our dreams may be more than just dreams. When we consistently have a feeling of peace or reassurance from an experience we feel was a communication attempt from our beloved deceased, we should not doubt the validity of our emotions. Trust in the truth of your intuition.

The living should not be worried about the presence of the near-earth deceased. Deceased we don't know are not watching our every move. They have their own work to do. Of course I am an exception to the previous sentence. I sometimes feel the attention of the deceased. Although I have good boundaries, deceased people I have known can reach me.

One morning I was up in my garden and smelled cigarette smoke. I looked around and no one was there. At that time I lived in an isolated area. The smoke was not likely to be coming from the neighbors. But the husband of an acquaintance had recently died of lung cancer. I decided to meditate later that day to see if it was Paul and we shared a good conversation. I asked him how he found me since I was sure he didn't know where I lived. He said he had followed me home from my job the evening before. Through several meditations he has become a friend and a great source of support for me. And yet the honesty of our current relationship would not have been possible if he were alive.

Another way the near-earth deceased can reach us is through our emotions. This is because emotion bypasses our reasoning intellect. When we feel an emotion that evokes thoughts of the deceased they may be nearby and trying to get through. When I first make friends with someone, I don't tell them right away that I am a psychic medium, I let them get to know me first. I have a friend who was glad to (eventually) learn I had some ability in the realm of the deceased.

My friend Jane had a coworker who died tragically. Ever since this woman's funeral Jane had been troubled with overwhelming anxiety. She had never felt like this before and it had started at the coworker's funeral, when Jane had her first panic attack. We worked together in meditation. It became clear that the emotions of this deceased woman were reverberating through my friend. It took several sessions while Jane tried to establish boundaries with this deceased woman. In our final meditation Jane told the deceased woman that she wanted and needed to be left alone. Jane is an open and sensitive person and this deceased acquaintance was trying to arc or ground her unpleasant emotions through Jane.

The use of emotion as a communication channel from the deceased is not arbitrary and is usually positive. Someone who has no relationship with a deceased person will not normally be a target for communication of any kind. The deceased have nothing to gain from spending energy trying to contact a complete stranger.

Although it is possible for the deceased to transmit negative feelings of bitterness, jealousy, anger or hatred toward the living, it takes tremendous energy for the deceased to do this. On the one hand, a healthy living person will resist a negative emotion especially when it comes out of nowhere. On the other hand, people who were evil in life don't function well in the afterlife. They are not highly energized and do not have the knowledge of how to energize themselves. Mentally and spiritually healthy people do not need to fear the deceased.

While I think many of us are capable of conscious communication with the deceased I don't advocate trying this in a casual or random way. There are practicing mediums all over the country. While all psychic mediums have different skill levels, I would much rather see the living be protected by some level of knowingness or discernment than none at all. Not many people can be sure that no unwanted negative spiritual influence will result from opening their mind to the deceased.

Having said that, I also feel communication gifts from beloved deceased we feel are close to us are not only possible but are a common occurrence. There is a book by Marianne Michaels called: A Second Chance To Say Goodbye (Infinity Publishing, 2002). I like the way she writes about how our relationship continues with the deceased. Marianne also provides some meditation tools for attempting conscious communication with deceased loved ones. While Marianne's motives and skills are pure, I have concerns about directly seeking communication with deceased loved ones. This may open the door to spiritual contamination by negative influences. I feel we should ask for signs and then accept and recognize their gifts to us but not try to force or demand communications. Contact with the spirit world is positive, relaxed, pure and God/Source oriented.

I am not open to just any or all random communication with the deceased. I am either asked to work by a friend or relative of the deceased or I have a reason to want to reach a particular individual. At times, as in the case of Paul, the deceased have a previous connection and a compelling reason to contact to me.

One day I was driving to town and I became aware (a deceased) someone was in the back seat of my car. On a straight stretch I felt a hand on my shoulder and mentally heard the words: call Sue. Then I knew who it was, the deceased husband of a woman I had worked with several times. I called her cell phone and it was a good thing I did, she was in dire straights in recovery from an operation and needed medical intervention, which I helped facilitate. Oh, did I mention, her husband had been a doctor?

The near-earth deceased have much less potential for affecting the living but the living can have profound effect on the deceased. This is because the living have much more inherent energy as compared to the amount of energy the newly deceased may have. While the amount of energy the deceased have is not fixed, like a tank of gasoline, many newly deceased have not yet learned how to energize themselves. The near-earth deceased have not yet come into the empowerment that complete assimilation and healing will make possible for them. We will see later in the book how unlimited energy becomes available to the deceased once they have moved into the higher levels.

Lets now consider our relationship with the deceased from our side of the mirror. There is so much that the living can do to help and benefit the near-earth deceased, both directly and indirectly from our side. The deceased listen to our conversations about them. They hear loved ones discuss the way that they died, how much they are missed or perhaps how our future will be different without them. The deceased may need to try to touch a loved one to find out that the living cannot feel their touch, or speak to us to learn we cannot hear them. In this way we help the deceased understand what is not possible for them anymore.

There are deceased who are not conscious for months after they die. When they do achieve self realization and wonder what happened to them we can inadvertently inform them of how and when they died. If we have a conversation about their death and they are conscious enough to perceive what we are saying, we could be informing the deceased, for the first time, what the manner of their death was. Sometimes I think we should have another memorial for deceased, say at the year anniversary of their death.

Once the deceased are conscious, they can look over anyone's shoulder while we read about the accident or read their obituary. In the case of sudden deaths they may not yet have a clear idea on what day or how they died. When we think of someone on the anniversary of their death, even year after year, we may supply information that helps them reach self realization. Remembering and talking about the deceased benefits them.

We can also help the near-earth deceased by holding in our mind an image of them when they were healthy and whole. We can actually influence their thinking in a positive way when we imagine them younger and healthy. Say our loved one dies in an automobile accident and our last image of them is perhaps dirty, bloody or disfigured. That image is so traumatic to us that we return to it again and again in our grief. Holding that image in our mind is not helpful to the deceased.

The tradition of an open casket at a wake can initiate a degree of healing for the living and also benefit the deceased. The final physical memory of a well dressed, groomed and peaceful body can replace, in the mind of the living, the image of their loved one in extremis. The deceased individual may perceive their body in the casket and not only understand they are now dead, but also use the clean and well dressed body as a starting point to improve their memory body. It is imperative, however, that the living remember the deceased when they were at their happiest, and healthiest. When people die, they are able to feel the most joyful they ever had in life most of the time.

The best way we help the deceased is by sending them our love and prayers. I cannot emphasize this point strongly enough. It is so incredibly important for the deceased that we send them love. Our love is energy that is transferred to them. When we pray for them, we are drawing on God/Source energy and sending that energy to them. Even to pray for someone we may not know personally benefits them by sending them energy. It may ease our grief when we know we are doing something valuable for the deceased through prayer or feeling love for them.

Many cultures have a tradition of praying for the deceased. Eastern religions have traditions where friends and relatives stay with the body in prayer for twenty-four hours and accompany the body to the cremation site. The living continue to pray and stay during the cremation process. Then deliberate prayers are said for the deceased for at least a year after the death. Most religions emphasize prayer for the deceased. The energy generated by these prayers is extraordinarily helpful.

The projection of sorrow or anger does not benefit the deceased. When I was finally able to communicate with my mother she asked me to stop calling her name so much. In my grief I was mentally calling her name over and over, not realizing it would bother her. Even if we are grief stricken at the loss of our loved one, we need to continue loving them, sending them our love, not our pain. It is a good thing for us to talk to a deceased loved one we feel nearby. Whether they are actually listening or not depends on how conscious they are. The conscious deceased are most always aware of family and friends who are thinking of them.

Beryl Markham told me she was aware of my admiration of her. I had the privilege of speaking with her about a year after she died. She was still in the near-earth deceased experience when we met.

Beryl Markham (1902-1986) was an accomplished writer, aviatrix and horsewoman. She was the first woman to fly solo over the Atlantic in 1936. Her autobiography West With the Night (North Point Press, San Francisco, 1942 and reprinted in paperback in 1983) is fascinating and stunning.

After I prepared myself in meditation, I heard her calling, "Over here dearie, over here." She was sitting on the porch of a house with a view that I sensed more than I saw. On the porch, which she called a veranda, was a square hassock with a woven reed seat. I sat facing her. She has changed her age and appeared in her early thirties. She said, "I decided to be your age so we could have a little chat. I have been expecting you. I am aware of the people who take a great interest in my life.

"I am so energized by the people who remember me, by their praise and interest. I can really feel my current popularity." She was referring to the fiftieth anniversary of her solo flight over the Atlantic from England to Cape Breton Island, in 1936. She continues, "My enjoyment of the recognition I have gotten since I died is clearer to me than the adulation I received after my flight."

I asked Beryl, "Do you understand now the choices that led you through such an incredible and interesting series of accomplishments in your life?" She answered, "The biggest accomplishment was keeping a roof over my head and food in my mouth. You can't imagine what that was like for me. It was a constant effort. There was a lot of terror and fear for how I would provide my daily sustenance. It was a fear that never let go of me for my entire life."

"I believe this fear started with the abandonment by my mother when I was at such a young age. Then my father abandoned me in different stages and in small ways. He even built a little house for me to live in when I was a teenager some distance from the main house. I interpreted this as rejection, a shutting out of me. I realized I was never as important to him as he was to me."

"I was terribly insecure throughout my life. None of my relationships could have scratched the surface of the terror I felt for my daily bread. There was a depth of me that no other person could penetrate. People thought that I was superficial but what they were dealing with was terror in my core that could not be assuaged by any person on earth."

"It was that terror that drove me. It was my handicap and my motivating force for so much of what I did in my life. I believe now that the greatness, the achievements that I sought were to somehow ease that terror and to win the love of my father. But it never did. There was never enough that I could do. He was the only one that could have released me from my fear. And there was nothing I could ever do in my life that could make him erase that fear from my very soul. He did not understand his importance to me."

"I do feel that if your parents do not give you comfort, security and love, there isn't anyone else in the world who can do it. Early childhood is a critical time. I was doomed to repeat history with my own son. However he had loving people around him, his grandmother in particular, who made him feel secure with her love. He can accept love to a greater depth than I ever could."

"When I think that I lived an entire life based on certain fears that were caused by other people I see that a great deal of my energy was wasted. I was not sufficient unto myself on so many levels. I squandered a tremendous amount of energy on that pain and fear."

"I am not advanced enough yet to know what the overall plan for that life was. I am staying close by the earth. I am encouraged by the remarkable admiration for my life and its achievements. I am very much reveling in that and dipping into places where people are interested in me, like you."

I asked her if there is anyone with her now. Beryl said, "This is a very individualistic time. At first my friend Tom was here. In fact he had been with me quite a bit in my old age, but I didn't realize it. When I died, I just flew right into his arms. We sorted everything out and then he had to go back to his own work."

"Now I feel so much acceptance and satisfaction from my own accomplishments. I am feeling so good within myself, more than I ever did in the best moments when I was in a body." I asked Beryl if she managed to keep a roof over herself in life. She laughed and said, "Yes, with the help of a lot of other people. I really shouldn't have worried so much but I couldn't help it. That kind of fear can eat you alive. Horses and dogs were the only creatures I could let into myself, let see me and know me. There is nothing I miss about being in a body."

"Of course I wrote West With the Night. (She was referring to some debate over the book's true author.) No one else could have. My husband suggested I keep some parts and leave others out, and what the best stories were. Sometimes I would dictate the stories to him. I would tell the chapters as if I was sitting at a campfire in Africa. That was a better way for me to write. But of course I

97

wrote that. It was my life. It is more satisfying to have left <u>West With the Night</u> than to have left my flight record. The book is art, not just a physical accomplishment. It was an artistic accomplishment and it will last."

I excused myself from Beryl because I had to get a glass of water. When I returned, she said, "I'm sorry, I should have offered you something." We laughed when I explained to her that the idea of a glass of water probably wouldn't have taken care of my dry throat.

I asked Beryl what she was going to do now. She said, "I don't know. I really enjoy being tuned into and using the energy that is coming from the (people on) the planet to me. I am also interested in keeping tabs on my grandchildren."

I said to Beryl that I had really wanted to meet her but I am also trying to understand what death and the afterlife is like. Beryl said, "My death was not difficult. I even willed it at the end. I went through an ambivalent phase when I was old, not caring if I lived or died. I wasn't able to focus on what I wanted for a while. But when I broke my hip I knew I'd be in bed longer than I cared to be so I willed myself to die. It is interesting how my will to live sustained me through so much of my life. I was in life threatening situations any number of times. I had a terrific bout with malaria that could have killed me if my will to live had not been so strong."

"I slipped gracefully into my death state. Death was not a trauma to me. I rose up out of my body and it looked as if my body was a cocoon. I remember thinking at the time I was like a butterfly coming out of a chrysalis. And I rose tall and graceful once more. I was really grateful for the feeling of a young body again. And then, of course, I hung around to make sure the old carcass was disposed of properly. Shortly after that there was a great celebration up in London I went up to. I stayed there watching my family."

"I really do not feel the continuity of myself through my family. The legacy I did leave on earth was my book, which was my life's story." Beryl then looked me right in the eyes and said, "Which was one hell of a story. But you are my first visitor. I've watched people but nobody has actually come to visit me." I explained to Beryl why she is not likely to get many visitors from earth.

I stood up and shook her hand, telling her again how much I admire her and honor her life. She said, "I wish more people felt that way about me, particularly when I was a child, but such is life. You are welcome to come and see me anytime. It was nice meeting you dearie." I had the visualization of a car down a little way from the porch. I mentally got into the car, and returned to my body.

There are many elements in Beryl's story that illustrate an ideal death and her ability to function in the near-earth deceased experience. She achieved self healing of her memory body at the instant of death. She changed her age easily. Her reality was so complete she didn't question the idea of visitors or the continuity of herself after death. She was as accomplished, brave and creative in the afterlife as she had been in life. And the best part was that she was not afraid anymore.

Chapter Seven

Moving On

There is no use having regrets.
You have to make the best of things
in your present, wherever you are
when your present is happening.

I once heard a radio program about the studies done with people who had lived to be over a hundred years old. In the speaker's opinion, the single most important trait all these people shared was the ability to adapt. Whatever problems they faced in life, they could work through and adapt to the changes in their lives. I'm willing to bet these people will adapt to their afterlife with ease.

In the chapter on The Newly Deceased we saw how the deceased learn to adapt to their new state. Once conscious, the newly deceased learn to heal by changing the age of their mentally projected memory body. They also learn how to change their location and move around while still near the earth. These are the baby steps to learning that we direct our own reality in the afterlife. The deceased learn there are choices that they can make. Once the deceased learn to make choices, one of the choices they can make is to rest in the near-earth deceased experience.

Many deceased will rest after they achieve self realization and are familiar with their memory body. Obviously the deceased do not have to rest their memory body; there is nothing about it that gets tired. What the deceased do need to rest and refresh from time to time is their mind. We rest our minds in life, by taking a walk, listening to music, reading or watching what can be termed "mindless" TV. In these ways we can shut down parts of our minds for a while.

Some deceased are a bit overwhelmed by thinking about their death or by the necessity to project or create their reality. In order to kick back from this effort they can choose to rest. After the deceased have oriented themselves to their new state of being and become aware of some of the possibilities here, such as travel, assimilation or healing, they may desire to go into a resting phase. The function of rest is then to slow down or stall experience. Resting for the deceased is as simple as just ceasing activity and can take place anytime in the afterlife.

When the deceased rest in the near-earth deceased experience, they do not leave this level of energy. Some deceased say they imagined a milky white cloud or blanket surrounds them while they rest. It really doesn't matter where on the planet they rest. But the deceased would not pick an area with a lot of activity, such as a subway station or a construction site. While hearing is not the issue, vibrations would have an impact on the memory body.

The deceased orient themselves to their location before they rest. Just as in life when we fall asleep, we orient ourselves in the place where we are sleeping. In the case of the bedroom we use each night, this is not important. But say we were at a hotel or had just moved, or rearranged the furniture in our bedroom. We might take a moment to look around and remember the placement of the bed, door and/or windows in the room before we close our eyes.

The deceased will also orient themselves to where they are located near the earth and where they are in reference to their mental processes. They might wish to keep in mind what they were last concerned with or what they were doing. Therefore, when they take up activity again, they have a reference point.

The deceased compare this rest to a dreamless sleep when they were in a body. When we are asleep, we are not doing anything with our conscious mind. But parts of the nervous system are still functioning, of course. If we hear a loud bang nearby, it will wake us up. There also remains some awareness in the mind of the deceased although they are not conscious. When they need to return to activity, while it may not be conscious or sensed in the case of a loud noise, there will be a gradual taking up of activity again. One deceased person explained it this way: his will to act ceased and then his will to act resumed.

When I think about how the resting deceased "wake up," I can compare that with my own habits on different mornings. On the days that I have to go to my job, I wake up well before the alarm clock goes off. I need to get the chores done, the inside animals settled, pack our lunches, change my clothes and get out the door. On the mornings I do not have to leave, I stay asleep until the alarm or a cat wakes me up. My will to act is different depending on the day's schedule. Even though I am asleep, something in my mind is keeping track of what I have to accomplish in the morning. I think some part of the deceased's mind holds a similar awareness of when it is time to become active again.

Slowing down experience is another form of resting for the deceased. They narrow or limit activity in order to rest. Ann, whom we met in the first chapter, was in a resting state for several months after she died. She said she still felt sleepy when she came up above ground, away from her body. Her mind had stayed with her body in order to rest. This was not so much avoidance of experience in the afterlife as it was a hesitation to progress within the afterlife. The afterlife is not a competition or a race. All our processes are individual; we can take all the time we want or need to rest.

If the near-earth deceased rest, they will continue with assimilation when they resume activity. The purpose of this phase of assimilation is not to learn to function on this level; they have learned that already through the process of self realization. Now, assimilation is to help them start to review their life in the way that it is possible near the earth.

This assimilation takes place in several ways for the near-earth deceased. It is common for the deceased to go to a location where an event happened or where they lived and think over what happened there when they were alive. It is also possible to be near people who were important to them or with whom they shared experience. We saw in the last chapter how they may be able to communicate with the living in some way. Communication is not the work of assimilation. Assimilation is reviewing the high points, the low points and the turning points in life.

The purpose of assimilation in this stage is to extract all the knowledge we can in the way that it is possible to review our life in the near-earth deceased experience. For example, emotion is more vivid for the deceased at this level than it will be in any succeeding phases of the afterlife. When a near-earth deceased person reviews events in their life, they can use emotion to process and assimilate these events. Feeling the anger, wonder, sadness or gratitude that they may not have felt surrounding a particular event or at a certain time in their life can help them assimilate what they might not have experienced emotionally at that time.

Memories triggered by the proximity to people and places are acute in the near-earth deceased experience. At times memories can engulf the deceased to such an extent that they tell me it is like traveling in time. They can focus, for as long as they wish, or be near the places that were important to them in life. The deceased can re-experience the emotions of these times, over and over if they wish to. They eventually reach a sense of completion or closure with these relationships or events.

The near-earth deceased can even explore the what-ifs; what if they hadn't met that person, what if they had made other choices, for example. The deceased can also assimilate what they regret about their life. No doubt, we will all have regrets when we think over our life. The deceased will assimilate these disappointments as well. But they do not emotionally dwell on them or, as the saying goes, beat themselves up about it. They realize they are not gaining anything from negative emotions and will eventually abandon repetitive non productive negative thinking.

The book, The Five People You Meet In Heaven, by Mitch Albom, (Hyperion Books) was made into a movie. It is about a newly deceased person in the process of assimilation. The movie's central character, Eddie, dies and five previously deceased people help him, in turn, to assimilate his life. Each of the five previously deceased brings the theme of forgiveness. Either they have forgiven Eddie something, or they need his forgiveness before they can move on.

Eddie finds each of his five previously deceased people in their particular heaven. These are examples of mentally created realities. The movie can help us understand the idea of assimilation and the mentally projected personal realities that can be created by the deceased. Through assimilation, Eddie changes the way he thinks about himself. He goes from feeling like a loser, thinking that he didn't do anything with his life, to understanding that his life did have meaning and he was connected to and benefitted many other people. I endorse the author's link between forgiveness and assimilation. Forgiveness of the self and others is the best path to understanding and assimilating life's hardest lessons.

Most deceased, at some point in the process of assimilation, will stop feeling like they are a victim of their death, or at the mercy of the deceased condition. They stop thinking about what they have lost when they dropped their body or ran out of time in life. They begin to feel that they are inhabiting their present.

Even though the near-earth deceased seem to be immersed in the past, assimilation of their life will lead them to a greater and greater awareness of their present. They become more interested in their present as they resolve the events and relationships in their life. Realizing they are in their present empowers them. It is only in the present that any of us can focus our will or direct our reality. Remember it is not absolutely necessary for the dying to mentally focus their will in order to leave their physical body, but it is necessary for the deceased to use their mental will power to progress in the afterlife.

I want to take a minute to review the four processes in which the deceased participate. These processes should not be all that foreign to us. After all, they are also a part of our physical life experience. Self realization in life is knowing who you are, in your present, as body, mind and spirit. Self realization after death is learning you are still in your present and that your personality, mind and soul still exist after death. Self realization continues in many stages of the afterlife within the challenges of increasingly intangible realities.

Assimilation is the translation of experience into knowledge. Assimilation is the mental digestion of life's events. Some people assimilate their life as they go along in it. If we think about what we learned from the painful events of life and try to forgive each other and our self, that is assimilation. If we think about the times when we were the happiest and what choices resulted in that happy event, we are assimilating our life. Assimilation, or the thinking about and learning from events in life, changes in the afterlife depending on what level of energy the deceased are inhabiting.

Healing is another ongoing process for the deceased as it is in life. We think of health and healing primarily as this applies to the physical body in life. But we can also heal mentally, spiritually, and emotionally in life and the afterlife. Healing can take different forms for the deceased in different stages in the afterlife.

There is a fourth process or task: progression. Some people, who enact a self-willed death, are deliberately progressing from life to the afterlife. Most of us just find ourselves out of body after death and begin to progress from the near-earth deceased experience.

However, in order to move on from the near-earth deceased experience the deceased are faced with a deliberate, self-willed and focused choice. This, then, is when many of the deceased first become engaged in the process of progression.

The next step, or progression, after the near-earth deceased experience is the earth portal transition. The earth portal is a layer of energy that connects the near-earth deceased experience to higher energy levels. The earth portal surrounds the planet much like our atmosphere above or beyond the near-earth deceased level of experience. I use the word portal as this connective experience is crossed or transited both by a soul entering physical at birth and by personalities leaving the close proximity to the earth at some point after death.

It seems gray because it is a transition or connective energy. We neither linger in the transition nor do we draw on or access any energy or experience from this layer. Of itself, the earth portal does not collect or give off energy.

Although we come through this transition at birth we don't remember it. To the souls coming in it is a one way street leading in toward the earth. Likewise, from their earliest experience perceiving the earth portal, the deceased understand this transition as a one way street, going outward or away from the earth.

Predeceased greeters may explain the earth portal as an irrevocable energy transition to the newly deceased. The earth portal is a transition the deceased can make anytime. This transition will dramatically change their afterlife experience.

The deceased can also glimpse the importance of this transition by "looking" back from the edge of this portal, back toward the earth. It is clear to the deceased that this portal leads away from the proximity to the planet. The earth portal transition is a change in energy levels, in experience and in possibilities for the deceased.

The deceased do not have to know where the portal will lead them. They will understand from contemplating this choice that it is the only choice they have to move on, move out or upward. The portal is appealing to those who have completed all the healing, assimilation and experience they desire near the earth. They perceive the other side of the portal as something better, brighter, with increased energy where they can expand or improve their experience.

In life we often undertake major transitions without being certain of the outcome. Examples of life transitions are moving, graduating or changing jobs, marriage or divorce. The will to progress and make the best of transitions in life prepares us for progression in the afterlife.

So while the deceased do not have to know exactly where this portal will lead them, they do have to make a conscious choice to accomplish this transition. This progression takes an act of will on their part.

As they focus their will and intent on the portal, an entrance will form in the gray energy. The entrance will resemble the opening of a tunnel. The will of the individual creates this opening. There is not just one tunnel, like the tunnels we would have on earth for car traffic. It is just universally perceived as a tunnel. It is our own private tunnel transition. The individual deceased's will creates their way to cross this area.

When the deceased are ready to move on, have spent sufficient time contemplating it and are sure this is the choice they want to make, then they enact the transition. Their will power generates sufficient personal energy to carry themselves through the portal. The deceased stay near the earth until they have formed the intent, the will, and the focus to enter and complete this transition. When we are near the earth, we know we are in the proximity of familiar places. We are able to feel, no matter how subtle, what we observe on earth. The near-earth deceased experience is more similar to physical life than any stage in the afterlife.

The near-earth deceased who are not able to focus their will to cross the earth portal are what we think of as ghosts. In general ghosts have lost the awareness of, or never had the knowledge of the earth portal transition. One traditional role of mediums is to help these earth bound individuals form the ability, the will and the knowledge sufficient to cross the earth portal.

There are many reasons why the deceased may not move on. Some deceased are simply fixated on the earth and do not look for light or higher possibilities to experience. Others are trapped here by an obsession with an issue they can no longer resolve with people or places that have moved on in time. A few deceased are mentally stuck in their beliefs and are stubbornly waiting for their beliefs to come true. Other deceased cannot forgive themselves for their mistakes or sins in life and believe they do not deserve to move on into the light which represents God/Source. Some deceased have bound themselves in ignorance, ignorance they cultivated through evil acts in life and so have diminished their choices in the afterlife.

If you are interested in ghosts I recommend a groundbreaking book written by a Polish woman, Wanda Pratnicka. It is titled: <u>Possessed by Ghosts</u>, Exorcism in the 21st Century (Centrum Publishers, 2002). My husband found Wanda's work on the internet after I had a brush with a demonic disincarnate. For the first time in my life, I saw this deceased man the way they are portrayed in the movie Ghost - as if he was alive and walking on the earth. His clothing was from the end of the 19th century. When he turned toward me he had no discernable face. Yet the malevolence of his energy directed at me was horrific. Within a few days I was able to spiritually recover myself but it was a lesson that will stay with me always. I had never before experienced the truly dangerous potential of my psychic work.

I agree with Mrs. Pratnicka that more and more deceased are becoming trapped here. That combined with the lack of spirituality, the God-less-ness in some of our society along with the use of drugs and alcohol opens more and more living humans to possession. I feel many of the atrocities committed here are by a living individual who has been joined by one or more demonic ghosts. Mrs. Pratnicka points out that many ghosts simply do not know they are dead. I agree that the vast majority of ghosts are not demonic but I now take greater care with my prayers and what I think of as my spiritual hygiene. Most ghosts are simply confused and can be helped to cross the earth portal which Mrs. Pratnicka calls death's curtain.

Once the will, focus and knowledge of the choice are there in the mind of the deceased the earth portal transition occurs quickly. The portal transition changes the deceased's experience. The deceased will still be aware of what is happening on the earth once they have crossed the earth portal. But they will not be able to feel what they are observing in the same way.

There is a refining or rarefying of the memory body that happens in the earth portal transition. This change in the memory body makes the memory of emotion and sensual experience more abstract. The deceased still have memory of sensual experience but these memories do not seem to reverberate within their vehicle any more. This is not a bad change. It is just different from the near-earth experience.

More than one deceased person told me that crossing the earth portal had felt more like death than leaving their physical body did. In life we are a bundle of energy sheaths or bodies, one of which of course is the physical body. The next lighter body is the astral body, sometimes called the emotional body. Our mind can also be considered a body as it is so connected to our species choice. I travel in my mental body or vehicle when I am in trance. When we come into manifestation we have carried our God/Source given intent in our soul or spirit, which is our core energy sheath or body. When any intent energy makes a species choice it dons the species mind orientation with emotional instincts and thought patterns. Then we don the physical body at birth. On the way back out we drop or shed the denser sheaths or bodies.

Even if the deceased do not anticipate the change in self perception that will happen crossing the earth portal in terms of the energy sheaths or bodies, this transition is also about saying good bye to the places on the planet that have been home. When the deceased understand that the earth portal is going to lead them away from earth, they take all the time they want to get a sense of closure. Some deceased cross the portal immediately after physical death. Others take their time to bid farewell to the places they loved on earth.

When I understood the significance of the earth portal transition, it had a profound impact on me. I may have the choice to ascend after this lifetime. If I never reincarnate and have another lifetime on earth, I think I will take a lot of time to say good bye to the natural world, to my fields and to my gardens, before I transit the earth portal. Those good-byes may not be easy.

Chapter Eight

Individual Work

When you know things are possible,
you can create anything for yourself.

After nearly thirty years of working as a practicing medium, I was given the gift of a completely new way of connecting the living and the deceased. A sixteen year old deceased client stonewalled me around our fifth reading and said: "I want my (still in physical) mother, get her out here, I know you can". Turns out, Nicole was right. I coached her mother with a series of visualizations and they had their first of several conscious reunions. They met in various imaginary scenes: in a swimming pool, at an apartment her mother had never been in, and a scene within her mother's bedroom. I have done this style of reading with a variety of clients now. Most say that it feels like they are imagining it, until their emotional reaction is so overwhelming that they accept the reunion is really happening. Thanks to Nicole, many of my living clients are able to touch the energy of their beloved deceased.

When I first started doing medium work, I used to visualize a spiritual house in which to meet with the deceased. The house in my imagination was Spanish style, with adobe walls and a tile roof. In meditation I would imagine myself going there. I saw it so clearly in my mind that I could walk through rooms, feel the weather outside, and see the gardens that I mentally created. I no longer use my spiritual house as a focusing tool. But the idea of an imaginary setting was not foreign to me when I learned that the deceased also mentally create environments to be in.

The most interesting mentally projected house I have ever visited was created by a grandmother who died in a car accident along with several other family members spanning three generations. In several meditations I met with each family member in various rooms within that imaginary house. These deceased were in different phases of self realization, healing and assimilation. But they were all together participating in the grandmother's projected house environment. I described the imaginary house in great detail to the living family members. They knew exactly what house the grandmother had modeled hers on, even though on earth, that house had been torn down years ago.

The levels of energy that we participate in beyond the earth portal are intangible. I acknowledge that what I write may seem like so much science fiction or fantasy. But for the deceased, and eventually for us as well, these energy platforms are real. The environments the deceased create with the energy are real. They are as real as physical environments and structures seem to us on earth. Both are energy forms but in different densities of energy.

There are many ways the near-earth deceased can have experiences with imaginary environments before they cross the earth portal. The near-earth deceased will stay near or go to particular physical places that have meaning to them. But they may have changed some aspect of that place mentally. Because I am communicating with them mentally I see the changes, not the actual site as it exists on earth. The park where I met Charlene, from the first chapter, was a mental projection of an environment, a picnic area near Lake Erie. She was newly deceased and in the near-earth deceased experience. I have no doubt we were near that physical location but it is not warm in January in Erie. I also met and spoke with her once when she was sitting in a mental projection of the Mustang convertible she had in life. Whether she was actually sitting in her car in her garage doesn't matter, that is the setting she projected to me. The next time we spoke she had created a field. We laid in "her" grass and watched "her" clouds passing over while we visited and played with her deceased dog, Fuzz. On another occasion we were in Florida.

These imaginary scenes can be considered thought projections. Thought forms exist also here on earth and psychics can perceive them. For example, have you ever crossed an intersection in your car and had the hair on your neck stand up? No doubt there was an accident at that location and the emotional echo was still there. A lot of ghost encounters in haunted houses are really thought forms or thought projections that have lingered in the house and sensitive people can perceive them.

The near-earth deceased work with thought forms when they go to the location on earth where a memory occurred. For example, a deceased man who was a soldier in World War II may re-experience his memory of landing on Normandy Beach while he is in that physical location. Yes, the geography is still there but the carrier ship is not. The physical beach may also be different because of erosion and certainly the memorial was not there in the year he is remembering. So the physical location may look different, but in his memory it looks as it did some sixty years ago. His mind is creating the environment from memory. He can project from memory the exact environment that existed when his platoon landed on Normandy Beach even if, out of body, he is visiting the physical location of Normandy Beach as it is today.

When I do soul rescue with suicide victims in the near-earth deceased experience, sometimes they are still within a mental projection of the manner of their death. I once worked with a young man who had hung himself. He thought he was still hanging in that building as it was his last tangible memory. His physical body had long since been removed, cremated and was shipped to another state. That scene did not exist in physical anymore. But he was within the mental projection of his memory. I had to get him beyond the projected environment he had created before we could do anything else.

When I ask to be with the deceased in a reading, the first visual clue is often a scene or an item within a scene. These projections of a place can start out being just a series of windows over a kitchen sink, a particular table, a specific chair or couch, a porch, etc. These scenes or items are recognized by my living client and begin to form the platform of the visualization within which I will communicate with my deceased client.

Not long ago I worked with a murder victim. This was my second meeting with her and she wanted us to meet in a small favorite restaurant she was remembering. I got the feeling she wanted to go out, like she would have with a girlfriend for a cup of coffee and a chat. Her projected restaurant felt real to me in the meditation. In the early stages of the afterlife most deceased fashion energy environments which resemble a physical location they were comfortable in. It does not matter whether or not they are actually in or near the physical location of the environment, it feel the same to them.

In later stages of the near-earth deceased experience, the deceased may distance themselves from the planet before they make the earth portal transition. Most are comfortable, by this stage, with the idea that the environment they inhabit is a projection of their mind. They may not realize the importance of these exercises when they are near the earth, but it is a good skill to have and be familiar with when they inhabit higher energies.

Once the earth portal transition is chosen and enacted, the deceased will observe and acquaint themselves with the immediate energy level they are on. They will perceive the energy they have to work with. Most deceased now will have experience within what I call healing energy levels after the earth portal. Deceased who know other choices they can make may well choose another level for experience or a higher gradient of the healing energy to work within. Most deceased find themselves in a level where the energy looks like vast sheets of colorful construction paper. There is a horizontal nature to this energy that suggests platforms to be on, platforms to build on, or surfaces. It is a soothingly colorful place, and not as crystalline bright or as fluorescent as are many of the higher or following levels of experience. The energy here reminds me of construction paper because it is soft, thick and is somewhat muted in its colors.

These healing levels of experience have also been called the plane of conceptual realties in several of my meditations. That is because there is no pre-existing environment presented to or seen by the deceased. The deceased have to make their own environment. They can easily build, mold or shape their own environment out of the energy available here.

This is the first level of energy after physical life where creativity can be easily applied and indeed has to be applied in the afterlife. As in every energy level there are gradients. Someone who is resting here may choose to inhabit a dense white softer energy within this plane, and someone who is actively working or healing may stay in the higher, relatively brighter levels. Within these planes of energy we can conceptualize or feel a type of tangible familiarity with what we mentally construct. It is an easy realm for deceased people to spend time on. The energy here is also what healers arc into or bring down to help heal others in physical

The thought forms the deceased construct and inhabit here are three dimensional and can be changed simply by willing it. In life we might think of this as having a vivid imagination. Except what we imagine in life doesn't instantly seem to exist around us. Self realization once again comes into play as the deceased learn how to direct reality in this level and type of energy.

The deceased have to become accustomed to how real their mental constructions seem here. This is because there is much more energy here than they had to work with near the earth. They may rapidly change scenes or settings before they learn to, with deliberation, create what they really want. This is like when they learned to move around near-earth, because they may have moved a lot faster than they really wanted to. The deceased here quickly learn here to control their mind, and must control their mind to a far greater degree than they have had to up until now.

I like to call this level beyond the earth portal the plane of conceptual heavens because the deceased here are going to imagine and project very positive or idealistic surroundings. They can form the environment of their personal heaven with the energy here. In the movie <u>What Dreams May Come</u>, Dr. Chris Nielson, played by Robin Williams, projected an environment based on one of his wife's paintings and walks within it. He doesn't realize he is creating this environment at first. There is a scene where his deceased dog joins him and he says: "oh no, I am in dog heaven!" Each and every deceased can form the environment of their personal heaven with the energy here.

I find that most of the thought constructions or environments the deceased create for themselves at this level resemble places they have lived in or visited on earth. It is common for the deceased to create their favorite house. Others create their favorite room from their home. Some create natural settings that had boundaries, such as an area in a grove of trees or a mountain hollow. I often work with deceased in these levels in the meditations and I enjoy their imaginary settings.

The deceased here are more energized than they were near the earth and they can, by concentrating positive mental energy, send a communication or gift of guidance to a living person on earth from this level. It is common for the beautiful gifts the living receive, of an enhanced bloom of a flower or guidance, to come from this and even higher energy levels the deceased inhabit.

That is because with a degree of assimilation comes the added energy of healing, so the deceased have more inherent personal energy to expend in these gifts to beloved family and friends on earth. While this arcing of energy gifts back to the living is common from the plane of conceptual heavens it is not the purpose of the work on this level.

So it is not true that deceased cannot be reached once they cross the earth portal. It is not true that they cannot reach us once they cross the earth portal. They serve as our guides from this and much more energized experience levels.

The purpose of this plane of conceptual heavens is for continuing the deceased experience in the way that it is possible here. Self realization continues with the challenges of creating reality within this level, a distance from our familiar planet. Self realization also entails the deceased becoming familiar with the changes in their sense of self; their vehicle.

In this phase of work we are in a more refined mental vehicle than we had in the near-earth deceased experience. A simple way to think about this is that when in physical we were the combination of the physical body, mind and spirit. Mind is our species identity, memory and emotion. Spirit entails not only our God/Source spark and our soul which can receive and intercept God/Source energy but also the intent we carried out from God/Source. An individual self knowing human on earth is a multidimensional combination of energies; we are bundles of different energies. At death the only body or energy form that is dropped from the individual is the physical body. Near the earth we are in a sensory memory body, which includes strong memories of the senses and emotions near the earth. Within the earth portal transition we shuck off the most dense of our light body, sometimes called the astral body so sensory-like experience is not as vividly felt. After the earth portal we are more purely mind and spirit. We are in what some deceased call a mental vehicle, which of course includes spirit. In this mental vehicle the memories of emotion and the senses do not affect us very much. This takes some getting used to.

Assimilation of the prior life is still the process of distilling experience into knowledge, except here the deceased are more dispassionate about life's events. This objectivity helps them have an emotional disassociation from their prior life and its events. This emotional detachment from life characterizes the process of assimilation in the plane of conceptual heavens. The deceased tend to view the events of their life as things that happened rather than an event that happened TO them. Life's events that held an emotional charge just don't evoke those feelings anymore. A more complete assimilation of the prior life is possible because of the lack of emotion or objectiveness the deceased can apply to the assimilation process.

Within the assimilation process a certain healing takes place. We may have regret or guilt over things we caused in life. The detachment here allows us to forgive ourselves and others more easily and be more at peace with some of our hard choices in life. In this way, self healing takes place through assimilation. The deceased, in every level of experience, are always able to draw in

God/Source energy as a means of healing and empowering themselves through prayer. More ambient energy is also available to the deceased in this level, so self empowerment and healing from life's hardships can be readily accomplished here.

When I asked one deceased person what they were working on at this level he answered, "I am still assimilating many of the sensory impressions, for example, the memory of what weather felt like, the colors in my favorite carpets and flavor of food. Those physical memories were easy to imagine with the sensory memory body near the earth. But here, what that felt like needs to be integrated over again into my mental vehicle." This was said by a person who had completed his first and only physical lifetime on earth so this level of work in the afterlife was new to him.

Once the deceased have achieved self realization on this level they are in their present point of power and can use this experience as they need to. They may choose to rest as soon as they are acquainted with this energy and what their self consists of here. In the near-earth experience we saw how a deceased person may rest by ceasing activity or simply by slowing activity down.

The ceasing of experience at this level resembles hibernation, a deep sleep more than just dozing or napping. In order to rest in the plane of conceptual heavens, the deceased would project a restful environment to be within. The deceased do not need to protect themselves from anything here. But because of the nature of this energy their mental projection is more substantial or less transparent than any post death experience they have had until now. Once the deceased create this barrier around them, they cease all activity.

The duration of hibernation may be quite short in terms of time as experienced in the physical world. Or it may be quite long within the same reference of our time. Someone who wishes to could chose to hibernate for several generations or a matter of seconds. Time has no relevance to the deceased processes. I can only surmise the deceased have some awareness even within hibernation, a sort of mental alarm clock set with their choice of when they wish to resume their individual work.

I cannot tell you what the subjective experience of hibernation is here. Hibernation is the most isolated of all the experiences in the afterlife. At one time I could not reach my paternal grandmother, who had been such a help to me as I was learning this work. I believe she was unavailable because she was in a hibernation phase or a resting phase.

What was really interesting to me is that she had left a recorded message, should I try to reach her. I realized we were not together in real time when the message, which played like a three dimensional video, was over and no further communication was possible. This experience made me sensitive as a medium, more able to distinguish real time communication as opposed to memories and memory based thought forms left by the deceased.

Even after years of validation by the living that I was indeed in touch with their deceased loved ones there was still one aspect of the afterlife that continued to bother me. It is this. No one reported to me there was anyone who guided their every step or who made their decisions for them in the afterlife. Orientation to the deceased state is facilitated by predeceased loved ones who greet us, who inform us that we are now deceased, who may explain our immediate location after death and the importance of the earth portal. Also, as in life, the deceased can tap their inner knowledge what we call intuition. I wanted to know why our advancement within the deceased experience is such an individual one. Why must we figure out so much of this on our own and make our own choices?

I am going to step aside now as a writer and let you read the answer I received to this question pretty much the way I recorded it in meditation. I receive these answers while in a light trance state similar to automatic writing, except I speak into a tape recorder. The answer came as follows:

Isn't that how it is in life? Isn't life a journey of learning how to live? Isn't life learning how to supply the basic necessities and then learning to choose meaningful work and love? In life you learn to think for yourself and make decisions at times of great loss or when you are faced with a problem that only you alone can solve.

It is not that much different in the afterlife. You know in your heart of hearts that you have to learn what life is all about and figure things out for yourself. When you are out of your physical body you still have to become familiar with your condition and learn what is possible in that reality. This is the way the process is set up so you can acquire self knowledge and learn to direct your experience.

What is really lacking when you die is the communication that is both an aid and a detriment to discovering who you are and deciding what you will do in life. After death, you cannot just mimic other people anymore. You don't have the peer group or authority persons to tell you what to do anymore. It is just your earthly perception of sociability and desire to communicate that makes the after life experience seem maybe barren or bleak because you do not constantly share experience with others as you do in life.

After death, the loneliness that you emotionally attach to physically being alone is gone. The capacity to feel the emotion of loneliness without a body is gone. You are aware there are other people around you. But it is simply a condition of the afterlife reality that you do most of the work in an individualistic sense. So the knack, the ability to make self-directed choices, has to be formed after death. It has to be, no matter how long this takes. (The end.)

For some people death begins a journey of finding out how to direct their mental and spiritual reality. We must understand the concept of directing our experience by our self. This knowledge, if not formed in life, will be acquired in the process of assimilation and self realization after death. Healing and progression are not available choices until you are able to form and direct your own experience. Energizing the choice to begin the deliberate steps leading to another lifetime on earth will not be possible unless you form the ability to direct your own experience.

In the light of this information all of our work in the afterlife could be called individual work. But after the earth portal is crossed most people choose to have an extremely private phase of assimilation and healing. The deceased have said that crossing the earth portal is a distancing not only from the proximity to the earth, but from a preoccupation with ongoing events on earth. They can now become preoccupied with themselves. Since this final phase of assimilation and healing of the prior life is the most solitary of all the afterlife experiences, I thought individual work was a good name for this phase.

Individual work will be chosen after the earth portal transition by the majority of the deceased. The deceased may well understand there are more energized states they can progress to. But they also know when they have not finished processing their previous lifetime experience. So a choice made at this juncture to do this work. We are not automatically propelled into the vacuum of individual work without willing this experience to happen.

The deceased participating in this plane of conceptual heavens understand and value being alone within their experience in order to think things over. They are in their present and using the opportunities this energy affords as they need or want to. They now concentrate on completing the assimilation and healing of their prior life.

Chapter Nine

Completion of the Prior Life

Sooner or later the deceased realize that
the state of being they are in
after death is the same state of being they
were in before birth.

Many years ago I was asked by friends to meditate and find out what I could about their oldest son. These friends are two of the kindest people I have ever met. Yet their young son exhibited behavior that was disconcerting at best and frightening at its worst. My friends were adamantly opposed to giving their son the recommended drugs. The son's fears and his aggressive rejection of adults particularly, was inexplicable. Once, on my way through their kitchen I said hi to this little boy and he screamed "stop looking at me." I then saw for myself how deeply confused he was.

I meditated by myself and information came to me. This child's last incarnation was somewhere in the Midwest and he was severely abused. He died as a result of the abuse. Yet he very much wanted to be alive during this point in our human history, and almost immediately reincarnated into his current body. He could not distinguish between the memories from his prior life and this lifetime. However, when he progressed beyond the age that he was when he was killed in his last lifetime he would do an emotional about face and be the normal child that my friends' love should have fostered all along.

Let me tell you, I was reluctant to even give the audio tape of my meditation to my friends, it all seemed too bizarre. After hearing the tape recording they felt it was the truth and were better able to help their son, knowing his suffering would end one day. I still know these friends and their son has turned out to be a happy, productive and mentally balanced young adult. Some years later I received an explanation of how this could happen.

It is possible any time after the deceased transit the earth portal for the deceased to enter pre-birth focus. Pre-birth focus leads to physical birth and another lifetime on earth. If the will, intent, focus or desire is great enough and sufficient personal energy is gathered at the plane of conceptual reality, a deceased person can make this self willed choice.

Although this boy could not have picked better parents, some deceased do enter pre-birth focus before they have assimilated and healed completely from their prior life. These personalities may not have taken the time to acquire the knowledge to make a good choice or at least an educated choice about their next physical incarnation. They may not have a clear plan for how they are going to use the opportunities in a body to advance in their personal evolution.

A hasty re-entry into life can create unnecessary difficulties for the personality. Most deceased take all the time and energy they can or need to complete every step in assimilating and healing the prior life. They take each phase of the afterlife in its time and prepare carefully for each next step.

Many of us probably did have past lives when we inhabited different bodies, at different times in history, in different countries, as the opposite sex and so on. To remember previous lives expands our self realization exponentially in life. The details we see can mirror similarities with our current lifetime. But more importantly we then understand that we have died before, continued with experience, and returned to life. Everything that is in this book on the afterlife is something you may have already experienced, perhaps several times. If this book strikes the chord of truth for you it is because you have lived before, died and transited the afterlife. Now you sit in life once again, reading about where you have been.

I think the concept of reincarnation and past life memories gets misunderstood because of a similar possibility. We can also have what are called paired or shared lives when we are in between physical lifetimes. We can choose this experience when we are within inter lifetime. Inter lifetime is the period after the prior life is completed and before pre-birth focus is chosen. It takes place at the human species consciousness pool or the city of light described in a following chapter. While we are within inter lifetime we may study the life of someone who interests us, watching that life so closely, often to the exclusion of any other experience, that those memories seem to be our own. We learn from that person's life as much as we do from any life we actually lived.

We can later unlock vivid, elaborate memories of that observed lifetime during a past life regression. But we may not have been in that body; we were not physically that person. This is why so many people think they were Napoleon or Marilyn Monroe. We can consider reincarnation memories as possibly just observed, paired or shared lifetimes. However, the learning we accomplished through observation of Napoleon or Marilyn Monroe is our own and can be valuable to remember.

Most of us have memories of other lifetimes if we care to unlock them. In a past life regression we can remember other lives normally with the guidance of a psychic or hypnotist. If the deceased are open to mental exploration in a more holistic way, they also can bring the knowledge from past lives into assimilation work at the plane of conceptual reality by searching their mind with this intent. While the memories of other lifetimes may not have interested the deceased when they were in life they are still useful. They can compare and catalogue their past lives with their most recent life experience. So there are interesting ways the deceased can assimilate their prior life by re-playing a "historical" event in their mind.

In a past life regression we do not remember every single day of that lifetime. We access the memories of high points, low points, emotionally charged events, people we may recognize in this lifetime, events we learned a lesson from and most often our physical death. I was fascinated to learn where, when and how we chose which memories from each life to keep with us. This process of distilling a life lived before this one, what we see in a past life regression, happens here at the plane of conceptual heavens during individual work.

The deceased at this level decide which lessons or experiences from the most recent or prior life they are going to keep in their memory. They will keep memories of what advanced them, what experiences contributed to their knowledge and the mistakes or poor judgment they do not wish to repeat. They sort out and discard the experiences that were not key to their development. They do keep memories of the other people who were important in the prior lifetime.

In life we dance with each other and a lot of the dances we perform are to assist and edify each other.

Some of our efforts may not directly aid our life purpose or learning. So this is the time when the deceased really sort out their memories. In this phase of assimilation the deceased decide which memories of their prior life contain the learning that contributed to their personal evolution.

When the deceased imagine a scene or scenario in their mind within individual work they know they are functioning completely within their own conjuring. The deceased do not come and go from this level in order to complete their individual work. They can imagine events at certain locations on earth but they do not actually go to that location as they might have when they were still near the earth. When they thought over life near the earth they could imagine and seem to feel a kind of inter-activeness, some feed back, because they could comprehend that location or place in the present. Within individual work all of experience takes place completely within their mind and feels like imagination.

They re-experience a scenario in order to look back on the prior life, its lessons, its twists and turns, the happenings, accidents, chance meetings and partings. They seek to find out their truth or the theme within the event. Once they decide what the lesson of an event was, they can assimilate the very same thing looking forward. They can imagine the scenario in terms of a possible future experience in a future life. This overlapping purpose to assimilation occurs very often.

In individual work the deceased are both finishing the prior life and also beginning to lay the foundation for a future life or learning. Assimilation here is not just thinking about something that happened in the prior lifetime. It is also asking the question of what if that something could happen differently in a future life. If I had that to play again how would I play it, how would I rework it? So the mental imagining that brings closure to the prior life can also begin the steps to planning another life.

Assimilation is a long word for thinking things through and finding our own truth in a situation or relationship. We use this process all the time in life to figure out things. Let's take a mundane example. Say we needed another automobile and are trying to decide whether to purchase a used or new car. We might have had a bad experience in the past buying a used car, or conversely a good experience with a used car- say a certain car purchased from a certain dealer. They now want to replicate that same good deal. All of this thinking is using past experience, combined with current conditions and using that to project a future outcome. So we assimilate our past, present and future in life, in order to make decisions all the time.

Of course the deceased are not concerned with cars anymore. They are pondering the larger themes of life, the attitudes that governed their choices. Did they do things out of fear- if so what were they afraid of? Did the major choices in life revolve around love? If so were some of these decisions a detriment to their learning? How was their time used in life? Were there periods of their life that were especially difficult and how long did it take to heal and forgive those times? Was there something left undone? These processes are so individual and private that we cannot really know what anyone's assimilation during individual work entails. But we can have an understanding of what the end result of this process will be.

When all the knowledge desired is gleaned from the prior life experience it is set in the deceased's mind and they will keep it with them. This completion process is like choosing which memories and knowledge we want to keep and then placing these memories in a jar. The prior life is then sealed as a jar would be sealed once it is filled. The deceased can always access those memories, that knowledge. They can take the memories of their jar, so to speak, and look them over. But nothing will ever be added to the jar that contains the distillation of their prior life.

I like this analogy particularly as it illustrated how the deceased archive their prior, or last lifetime memories, but can also have memories from past, or previous lifetimes with them as well. They may keep their past, or previous to the last, lifetime memories in different jars, so to speak. But these jars are still with them and able to be remembered at any point. When we have a past life regression we are looking over the memories we stored in our mind from a previous particular lifetime that we archived when we were in this very stage of our afterlife.

As the deceased are satisfied that they have gleaned all the knowledge possible to extract from events, the prior life becomes less and less important. Until this point in the afterlife the deceased think of themselves as the name they had in their prior life, as the person they were. After assimilation and healing of the prior life is complete, the deceased begin to form an identity that has less to do with who they were in their

141

previous life and more as simply a person who is continuing experience.

When I explored my past lives I began to understand this concept. I began to relate to myself as the continuation of individual experience rather than just the personality and the body I am in this time. For the deceased, this change in self identity comes with the completion of individual work at the level of conceptual reality. It is key to progressing beyond this level of experience.

Chapter Ten

The Threshold of Choice

You cannot say there is
one way or one path
for everyone in the afterlife.

I'm always curious about how other people depict the afterlife. I find a kernel of a true possibility in nearly every book or movie. There are many personal heavens, many personal hells and many possible afterlife experiences in between. What bothers me is anyone who says they have the only true answer, that there is only one way that everyone will experience the afterlife. No one can really say what anyone's continuing reality will be upon death because it has been and is created by each individual as they go along.

Everything we can imagine after death is possible to experience to some extent if only within our own mental reality. Even a temporary ceasing of experience can be brought about in an individual who dies with a strong enough belief that death is like the blowing out of a candle. That was their truth in life and that will be their truth in the afterlife until something changes it. The afterlife is a self directed mental and spiritual experience.

What I have been presenting to you are the possible choices we will have to enact the tasks of self realization, assimilation, healing and progression. Those choices can be enacted in gradients of energy, energy levels or energy realities that are progressive. I can only tell you that this is the work we can choose to do after death and these are the places where we can choose to do the work. What you choose from the options you see for yourself is up to you. It is the choices, more than the afterlife, I am describing, hopefully, in a logical and sequential way.

As we try to discover more choices for ourselves and enact the highest possibilities available to us in our afterlife, our choices become broader, more varied and more downright fun. Once the deceased are satisfied they have assimilated their prior life as best they can and they are willing to move on from it they have more experiences to choose from, more choices to make.

Once in a meditation, I asked to understand where my spiritual house was located. I received a long essay on the levels of healing energy as an answer. The plane of conceptual heavens or conceptual reality, where individual work takes place, is one of these healing levels of energy. I was using this healing energy when I worked in that spiritual house.

As it turns out there are healing energies, gradients or different types of healing energy to and through all of existence. These energies can be drawn on or drawn in at any stage of life or the afterlife. These energies improve or enhance our life or experience. In other words these energies make us better. The human way to interpret or understand getting better is healing. Healing is the word I assigned to these energy levels. It may not be the most correct word, but it is the most descriptive and accurate one I have found so far.

The fact that the healing energy is to and through all of experience is important to understand. In life we can use prayer or positive imagery to draw healing energy into our body. There are healers here on earth that can channel and transfer this energy to others here. Most of the types or gradients of this energy are mentally accessible here on earth as well as at any point in the afterlife. The deceased make use of healing energy.

We would comprehend the densest quality healing energy as a milky yet luminous fog type experience. I think of this energy as thick clouds lit by the sun. When one draws in and feels immersed in this healing energy it may seem like we are in a cocoon. We feel its softness; we feel safe, protected and isolated from our pain or troubles. At any point in life or the afterlife this experience is available to us by changing our mental focus through prayer or meditation.

A more energized type of healing energy is the horizontal kind where individual work and the completion of the prior life takes place. The plane of conceptual reality is the healing level that is specific to our planet, to physical here. Often when I speak with or work with the deceased we create a platform as a beginning to sort out experience using this horizontal energy. Camilla's beige disk in the Soul Rescue chapter was on this energy level.

A higher, more energized type of this healing energy is bright and colorful like spray paint sprayed in the sun filled air. The color sticks to you as Leo says in Chapter Thirteen. One higher level has more form where the colorful snow crystals seem to have their own architecture. One level exists where color is dancing in a musical way. There are many higher, clearer, brighter and even more energized types of healing energies and experience levels which, I am told, are closer to the God/Source realities.

So, the deceased within the plane of conceptual heavens are already in healing energy. The individual work of assimilation always results in some healing from the prior life. After the completion of the assimilation of the prior life, the deceased will contemplate their need for a more deliberate healing experience. Most deceased, as their individual work draws to a close, understand they require additional energy. The deceased who choose to mentally participate in the higher healing energies overcome or heal any lingering effects of the prior life. Another reason for this deliberate healing choice is to fuel up, so to speak, for their next step. The healing energies are not a reward for completing assimilation of the prior life. In fact, accessing the healing energy is still considered part of individual work.

The drawing on of this healing energy is still an individual choice for the deceased. The deceased who have had difficult lives may keep their mind focused on this color/light/musical energy for a prolonged period. The duration of mentally dwelling in and the drawing in of this healing energy does not correspond to the length of the prior life, but it does correspond to the need for healing from life's traumas.

The deceased at this stage do not actually go into these higher energy experiences even though some say they feel as if they do. It is more accurate to say they stayed within their own environment and formed a bridge to it with their mind, the way we would imagine the arcing of an electric current. They then integrate the healing energy into their memory, mind and soul.

The deceased say this healing energy is able to be drawn in and integrated within what they think of as their mental and spiritual vehicle. Although they have the memory of the body they had in the prior life they say they are more just the energy of their personality at this point. But as one woman said: "We can always harken back into a bodily form and clothe our self with the memory of the body from the prior life. We can be whatever age is desired for the most effective healing."

Part of this final healing from the prior life is to learn to be joyful again, as the ability for emotion was left in the near-earth level. The deceased do not recover the emotional ability to react to things they consider good or bad. Feelings now become self generated and originate completely from the self. So obviously these feelings are all positive in nature. The deceased can and will create happiness and playfulness within themselves.

The deceased say that when they mentally focused on this self healing and empowerment they began to be social again. "Not only do we begin to interact with other people here but we can choose to interact with the personalities of other life forms as well. We will feel the unity with other people and life forms here and we learn to incorporate this higher energy into our environments."

The deceased are really beyond the impact of their prior or previous lifetime when they are accessing the healing energy and grace at this juncture. They become healed of the sentimentality, healed of the emotional attachment to the events in the prior life, they are healed of any longing for the past. They have rested all they need to through hibernation and are ready to progress.

When the deceased desire to progress from the completion of healing or simply desire to move on, their focus is drawn to the upper or outer edge of the plane of conceptual reality. I call this edge the threshold of choice. The will to progress and move on will make them aware of the threshold of choice.

The threshold of choice is the true stepping off point from the prior life. It is a place where the deceased pause and ponder what is next for them. The threshold of choice appears to me to be a lip or the edge of the plane of conceptual heavens. Beyond the edge there is a gap in energy, a lightless void. The deceased here realize there is no process or activity inherent at this lip or edge. They are not continuing meaningful experience here. Eventually they will be compelled to make a change or choice.

The newly deceased were helped out of their body when they died by leading visualizations and disincarnate greeters. The earth portal transition was clearly perceived as a tunnel. The threshold of choice, and the void beyond is a further challenge to their self-directed will. This transition also requires a deliberate and concentrated mental focus. But by now, the idea of a transition in energy is familiar to the deceased.

From the point of view of being in a body we can look at this transition as a third death. The first death was the dropping of the physical body. The second is the tunnel transition away from the proximity to the planet. This third transition signifies the prior life is truly ended.

I am only aware of two choices that can be made here. The deceased may continue in inter lifetime with the potential for another lifetime in physical. Or they may move on in the process of ascension. Some deceased have the knowledge and the will to ascend. These ascending deceased have understood that choice long before they arrive at this juncture. Ascension was their intent throughout life and the afterlife. Enlightenment and the orientation toward ascension does not happen at the instant of death, it is nurtured in physical life.

There are also deceased who have the knowledge to ascend but deliberately choose to continue with inter lifetime experience. Whatever the choice, this is the turning point from the prior life.

From the threshold of choice all the deceased can perceive a radiance some distance across the void. The deceased do not need to know what this radiance is. It is appealing to those contemplating it. It is understood that it is the next step and better than staying at the threshold forever. Many deceased are only aware of the one choice, this light that beckons across the void.

The deceased gravitate toward the radiance by keeping their mind focused on it. As they move toward it, it looks like a city of light floating in the void. What they are seeing is the edge of this level of energy. As they get closer, they may think it is heaven because it is so much more energized than the void surrounding it. Also, it reminds them of heaven because there are gateways that resemble the mythical pearly gates. These gates are not there to exclude anyone. They are entry ways for anyone who is self willed or desires to be admitted.

This city of light is not heaven. Although after the long individual work, it may seem like heaven with its interesting sights, the stimulation of learning and the diversity of people here. The city of light is the human species consciousness pool. All of human experience is here to learn from. This is the level of energy where inter lifetime takes place.

The choice to continue in life and have inter lifetime at the city of light and the possibility of reincarnation is not a lesser choice than ascension. Just because the choice to stay within the potential for another physical lifetime is not the choice to ascend does not make it a wrong or descending choice. Both are positive choices, positive for the individual. The choice to ascend will ultimately lead to the complete unity with God/Source and the end of the ego component of self knowing. To a lot of people relinquishing the human ego does not sound like a positive choice at all. But there is no judgement. There are no judgment calls. There are just choices.

Chapter Eleven

Inter Lifetime

After individual work is complete you go to a hub, a meeting place far away from planetary influences. This is a social place where news is shared and work is not self centered. It is a place of learning where people plan their next life.

The Wizard of Oz, a book written by L. Frank Blum, was made into the famous movie in 1938. As I learned about the human species consciousness pool I was amused about how many of the elements of the The Wizard of Oz resembled parts of this level of experience.

Across the void from the threshold of choice the gleaming city off in the distance seems like Oz. Before Dorothy looks behind the curtain, the wizard is similar to the figureheads that represent topics of learning here. The energy at this level is yellow/gold in color - yes, the roads here glow with yellow energy. Every human on earth has come through the human species consciousness pool on the journey into physical life. The similarities between Oz and the human species consciousness pool may be one reason why the book and movie are such enduring classics. Some part of our mind remembers this place.

The deceased call the human species consciousness pool different things. Some deceased call it the hub city because meridians of human experience intersect here. The meridians seem like lines of energy and radiate toward the species consciousness pool like the spokes of a wheel.

Others refer to it as the city of light, which is my favorite name for it. In reality it is the human species consciousness pool, where every possibility for every human, everywhere humans exist, is contained as information. It is where every theme of every aspect of human life and culture can be studied. The history of the human race is also stored here. The future possibilities for the evolution of the human species can also be explored here.

I've been to this level many times in my life. I have roughly a thousand pages of channeled material that I downloaded and transcribed from figureheads or teachers at this level. Most of that channeled work I did in the 1980s. It takes a fair bit of concentration to reach into this level, but it is so worth it for the knowledge.

The human species consciousness pool looks like a city because the human idea of organization is architecture. Humans also define space with architecture. But the function of these buildings is not shelter. There is no weather. The difference in perceived size or scale of the building corresponds to the scale of the topic or themes they encompass. There are ribbons of energy between the architecture, resembling roads. It is a plane of energy, the buildings exist on a horizontal plane or surface.

When the deceased will or direct themselves toward the city of light from the threshold of choice, they will become aware of gateways. They resemble large archways. There are gatekeepers and greeters who welcome and direct the incoming deceased.

The gatekeepers are the greeters for this level. They usher the deceased a little way into the energy sphere or experience level and help them orient to the sheer vastness and the incomprehensible amount of energy inherent here. New arrivals can stay near their gatekeeper or greeter until they are acclimated to the energy here. Near these entrances we can mentally call to predeceased friends, ancestors or group members we wish to reunite with and may join a soul group for a while.

Many other psychics, in trance or meditation have been to this level of experience. Some psychics say that the deceased entering this level are sorted, grouped and moved in groups to different areas of this vast experience level. I would not rule this possibility out although I have not seen this, nor has anyone mentioned it to me. If this grouping exists, I believe it is voluntary. I had no trouble moving into and through the city by myself.

The deceased's earliest participation in this level is, once again, the self realization necessary to function here. Self realization at this level is quite different from their previous afterlife self awareness, and most interesting. By now the deceased have reached a self identity having less to do with who they were in their prior life on earth and more to do with just being a human continuing experience. The prior life is over, it is healed and sealed. They are not yet focused on reincarnation or pre-birth choices. They are in between lives. As they approach and enter the city of light they begin inter lifetime.

The deceased at the city of light are less what we would think of as a personality and more just an individual mind and soul. Their personality is linked to the person they were in a prior life. The most tangible expression of selfhood at this level is the species identity: being simply a human. There is no racial or gender distinction here.

People here are more the same than they are different. Think of a school of fish. We can tell the fish are individuals yet the similarities between the fish are greater than the differences. If I had to describe what the energy dynamic of a human on this level looks like I would say we look like perceivable energy forms the size and shapes of humans.

Humans here can tell where the boundary of another person exists. We do not merge, nor is there an overlap of individual energy here. Of course the deceased remember who they were in the prior life. If the deceased at any time at this level wish to share or show their prior identity and personality they can project, from their mind, who they were and what they looked like. It is like flashing an identity badge. But the deceased do not have to maintain that projection in order to feel like themselves.

It is hard enough for us to understand how we continue without our physical body, which we left at death. Then we leave the emotion and sensory memory possible near the earth in the earth portal transition. At the threshold of choice we have stripped away who we were in our prior life and sealed it in memory. Now at this level we are simply a human mind with selected memories and the God/Source component of our soul. But these challenges of self realization in the afterlife are gradual. When the deceased reach this phase they will understand their selfhood.

We can't think of the human species consciousness pool as a fixed size. It is not like New York City, a fixed geographical size defined on a map. So to think of it as a city, even the largest city on earth, even the whole of North and South America as being one city does not begin to approach the scale of this place. It is indescribably vast and elastic in its boundaries.

As the deceased learn to energize themselves and move around at this level they also learn of the possibilities here. They start to make choices within those possibilities. One of the possibilities is to create your own environment or set up housekeeping by a thought construction of whatever you desire. Since everyone here creates their ideal, there is no prime real estate and no slums, although one person's palace may hold no appeal for someone else.

One woman here told me a vast amount of space exists at this level where people live in the projection of every possible style of house or type of dwelling. There are condos and high rises, igloos, houses, tents, yurts, huts etc. No one is forced to dwell in any particular construction, it is completely a matter of choice.

She also said that it is quite common for people to settle near people they have known in life. But this level is not like on earth where we try to help, meddle or interfere with someone else's experience. We don't monitor or keep tabs on neighbors or even people we knew in life. There is no danger here, no weather nor need for food. Most people stay within their house, home or dwelling even though they can and may change the enclosing environment at will for themselves.

Everyone understands that they are not to infringe on another human. This is so different from our social interaction on earth where we do influence the people around us. We are so interconnected on earth, even anonymously, say, when we are stuck in a traffic jam and chatting with the driver in the car next to us.

One person here described social interaction this way. He said, we don't try to interfere or change the course of anyone else's experience at the hub city. We abide here, we develop, we are here to learn. There is no ability for anyone else to affect anything besides their own activities.

Another woman said that the people you are seeking (ancestors or old friends, for example) may or may not be here. But if you find them you don't merge, intermingle energy or have any effect on them. You can meet, visit and exchange stories. This is also true of neighbors at this level. Neighbors are deceased who have their personal mental projection of a dwelling adjacent to another human's dwelling. Of course, moving or changing your dwelling is easy.

There are group settings here for humans who were not self knowing in life. One example is babies who died and did not achieve self realization in life. Another hive, or group setting occurs with the mentally disabled from birth and throughout life. At death these personalities are absorbed into a group dynamic where the projected house is not of their own making. There are helpers in these scenarios but the helpers still do not impose their will on any members of the group.

Although I haven't specifically seen this, I wouldn't rule out the possible choice to form a group with other deceased who shared a particular experience, such as murder or suicide victims. Other groups may form that have had a specific religious affiliation. Humans here may form groups to study a culture, time period, or share a fascination they had with a particular theme when in life. There would be no reason why we could not agree to form groups as long as we did not interfere with or influence other members of the group.

My first visit to the city of light was when I asked to be with Ann, a childhood friend. We met Ann in Chapter One. I would like, here, to have more of Ann's meditation which describes what she does here at the city of light. This meditation with Ann was the first time I had reached the city of light with my work.

In meditation I came to a gate and was met by a doorman of sorts. He already seemed to be aware that I was trying to reach Ann. I took his arm and we moved from a navy blue space into a brightly lit place. The light didn't seem to be coming from any one source. At first I saw a courtyard surrounded by buildings. The doorman or gate keeper said his only function was to usher me through the gate and I should feel comfortable exploring this place by myself. He told me I had the power and ability in my mind to go wherever I wanted to. I thanked him and he turned away from me.

I renewed my intent to be with Ann. I then found myself up above all these energy constructions that looked like buildings. I decided to stand on a roof and call out to Ann. I felt when Ann came and had a glimpse of a small pox scar she had under her left eyebrow when I knew her as a child. I threw white light on her and her image became clearer. We greeted and hugged each other.

I asked her what this place was. She said, "This place is like a city except it is much more of a big neighborhood. Everyone has a feeling of equality, even if some people are more developed than others. There is no competition. There is no crime. There is no overcrowding or hassles or anything. But there is a lot of activity. I'm very busy myself and people here have a lot of high energy."

"I have been here a long time. I do work with people who died as babies, kind of a cosmic kindergarten, (we laugh). I could choose to do other things, and maybe I will at some point. I went to a counselor before I was able to work with baby souls, the baby people. I had to petition to do this and show that I was interested in doing this."

I asked her how she got here. She replied, "when I left the farm some time after my death I went to another phase of existence. I went to a place to experience different color realities. This is the only way I can describe it. I was in a fluorescent pink and green place. It was a place of healing where I learned to be happy again. I had released myself from the earth experience but I had to learn to be happy again."

"That place was really beautiful. I learned to feel joyful, to feel good about myself because I had been unhappy for a long time. There I learned to play and splash around in this color. It was a very individual thing. I stayed there until I felt wholeness in myself. That place was fairly close to this hub(city)."

"After that I was ready to socialize again and feel OK about being away from the earth. I am having a ball at the hub and I don't plan on going anywhere else soon. I have found a purposeful occupation here. The energy is constant here. We don't have to sleep or eat. You don't get tired. You share energy up here by sharing a kind of tone or essence of yourself with other people."

I asked her if she is going to incarnate again. Ann answered, "no, I have no interest in that at this time. I have a room that I can materialize for myself to be in. If I need privacy or to be alone I simply create this for myself and stay within it." She is showing me a box around herself. She looks tireless and has wonderful energy. We continued talking for a while about her family and the time we had together as children before I hugged her and returned to my body. Ann called the city of light the hub. It was interesting to see how she described her healing after assimilation of her prior life. It was also fascinating to hear the way she described interaction with other people here. She saw this level of experience as an end in itself.

In life, each of us only experiences what we interact with in our present. This is true of the afterlife. Our experience is where we are, what we are doing and what is surrounding us. We are in our present no matter what stage of life or the afterlife we are participating in. An individual in the city of light continues to choose how they will use their present experience.

One way to look at these choices is where activity takes place. The deceased can inhabit their own thought projection, their home base. They may rest, or stall activities in this private setting. They may also think about the information they have acquired or plan their next mental or social adventure.

They can also socialize, leaving their dwelling place in order to interact with people they knew on earth as well as meeting others. I'm sure people can entertain here, inviting another into their dwelling. One person said that you have the basic instinct when you are near someone else here whether its a person you want to pursue or not. Not that you can know everything about them, but you get a feeling whether they are someone you want to communicate with. If they want to meet you, you swap stories.

The most common activities here are exploring and learning. I know this sounds like school, but as the deceased begin to realize, the possibilities here are anything but boring. Take, for example, the next time I found myself at the city of light. It was the result of asking a question.

In meditation I had asked the general question of why does evil exist. I mentally traveled to an enormous lecture hall, took a seat and spoke what I was hearing. I guess I didn't exactly blend in with my mental vehicle. I felt the curiosity of the people around me, but I pretended to know where I was and what I was doing. I have been to this level more than a dozen times in the course of my work since then. My next book, will combine essays downloaded from the human species consciousness pool with the learning paths we can follow here in life.

These large buildings, like an auditorium, function as containers of information on specific topics, or themes. The more general the question or comprehensive the theme, the larger the library, hall or auditorium. Several other psychics have seen this level as a vast library.

All of human experience through the ages, in every culture from everywhere humans have ever existed is available to explore on every level of practice or expertise. The deceased could spend an eternity sampling different human experiences here, but usually start off

164

with the themes of the prior life and gradually prioritize their interests.

Mind and manipulation are huge topics of research here particularly as expressed by a human. The ability for speech and the structure of the human hand are the prominent characteristics of our species. While tool making and abstract communication are not unique to humans, the language of mathematics and physics is. Study of the capabilities of the human mind can simply be the range of development of the human mind over a lifetime. Manipulation is anything we direct our hands to do with our mind. The list is virtually endless, everything from manufacturing, to gardening, to magic, to cooking, to energy storage is manipulation of material on earth.

The human body is another major theme. Some humans are fascinated by what the body can accomplish. Sports, stamina, dance, health and hygiene, or even the simple progression of physical function as we age may be studied. The deceased may be particularly interested in what illness or disability they had in their prior life. The implications of a gender choice is a branch of the human body theme. I have suffered and died in past lives from lack of antibiotics. In pre-birth focus I'm sure I did not want to come into life again until antibiotics existed- well, that and hot showers.

Emotion is another strong human theme. Some deceased want to understand the emotions that may have hampered progress in life. Others may not have experienced emotion as intensely as they would have liked. Still others want to simply understand how emotion reverberates on the mind and body. Emotion is not unique to our species but the way emotions interact with our brain and body is of interest.

Moral, religious or ethical themes can also be explored. These are particularly interesting within cultures in which we did not live. Social issues such as politics, authority, justice, hierarchy and class systems are explored, from the setting of a kindergarten class all the way to the global economy. The ways humans interact with other humans, such as parenting and family dynamics in all their sub topics are available.

Communication themes such as media, writing, and all the arts both from a historical and futuristic vantage are available here. Many are interested in aspects of our planet such as weather, pollution, natural resources and the evolution of the planetary systems.

As I mentioned before there were, are and will be other human populations within other star systems in the universe. We can explore other systems' cultures as well during inter lifetime. Think of all the cultures we have just on this planet. Some seem like other worlds, so different are the customs and beliefs. Now imagine being able to access the geography and anthropology of a different planet. Boggles the mind, doesn't it?

I believe there are many manifesting levels that we can incarnate within other than the density of physical materialization in order to fulfill our God/Source given intent. The city of light may well be a place to study these opportunities as well. I cannot say this with the authority of direct knowledge but it stands to reason. We all have to come through this level because of our species choice before we move on to a manifesting phase.

Since all of human experience is stored here, this includes the hedonistic, degrading and evil activities humans are capable of. As strange as it may be, violence, torture, self destructiveness, all of the negative activities humans participate in are also here to tap into. It would be misleading to say that all information here is cheerful or positive. The deceased have to choose what they are going to view and learn about in inter lifetime. Humans may not be the only species in the universe capable of negative creativity as well as positive creativity, but since we embody the potential for both good and evil this knowledge has to be available as well.

Particularly interesting to me was that the study or exploration of the themes by the deceased here happens exactly the way it does for me. In meditation, I arc my mind to this level with intent to recover information on a certain theme or topic. In inter lifetime the humans here also simply change their mental focus with intent to explore or study a topic. They do not have to leave their projected environment, just as my body does not have to leave my home. Although they can move around this level of energy they do not have to in order to access information. When I understood this, all I could think of was the analogy of us here on earth surfing the internet. Through the computer we access information and meet and socialize with people all the time without leaving our home. The deceased can mentally reach out from their own thought projection and draw on information available here.

A hierarchy of sorts exists here corresponding to who humans in inter lifetime go to for help and advice. The figureheads I have mentioned before represent topics or themes of study. They are mythical figures that provide a mental focus for learning. They seem to dispense the information. They remind me of Jung's archetypes. Personally, I don't think of these figureheads as humans, even though we perceive them in a human form. For one thing they are much larger than the rest of us. Perhaps their size is related to the knowledge they represent. They are self knowing individuals and I feel they are higher beings who were never humans on earth.

There are also consolers at this level. Newly arriving deceased can choose to join group settings to begin self realization with a consoler. Say, for example, victims of suicide, murder or drug addictions may join a group with a consoler in participate the initial stages of experience.

These guides or consolers teach and help the deceased but do not make choices for them. I feel the consolers did have a human life in physical at least once but are also wise and advanced human beings. When I meditate with my own life consoler I draw information from this level. Consolers guide and inform anyone who seeks help here.

When I finally understood a little of what this level of experience encompasses, the lack of other species was upsetting to me. I did not see any trees, plants or other animals here. I understood the city of light consists of what humans do. I found this level most unappealing at first as my joy in life is gardening and animals.

Once, in a recent meditation, I asked to be with my paternal grandmother in order to ask about this. I found her in her thought construction with her cat and plants. We were in a projection of a house she once lived in with this cat and these plants. I have been told that anyone here can blossom a memory projection of trees and animals you knew or were familiar with in life. But I have to wonder how gratifying or fulfilling that memory based experience is.

I already knew that we can visit the very edges of other species consciousness pools. These are parallel to the human species consciousness pool. We can study and observe other life forms. Here are a few things I was able to observe at the edge of ordinary house cat consciousness. To a cat every horizontal plane in a house is what we would think of as a floor. The outside of the house to a cat is like a different universe. Cat to cat recognition is so foreign to us I can't even describe it. They have a much different concept of height relative to their size than we do. Anyone in inter lifetime can shift their focus in a sideways direction to another species consciousness and learn at their gateways. I have a friend who channels information from horse consciousness in order to help heal horses.

I believe the human species consciousness pool is the intuitive information source for the geniuses on the earth. Many of the inventors, artists, scientists, and people who have original ideas and are considered ahead of their time, are tapping into the knowledge here in the creative process. Many psychics also tap information from the human species consciousness pool.

I feel so lucky to be on planet earth at the same time as Sylvia Browne. One of her books is <u>Adventures of a Psychic</u>, (Hay House, 1998). Sylvia channels Francine, her spirit guide. Francine says we are reunited with our pets at this level. From my own work, I understood that we will be reunited with all species and life forms in ascension. I was incredibly relieved to hear that being with our deceased pets is possible at this level as it is in the near-earth deceased experience.

Francine also describes the hierarchy of the city of light in a comprehensive way. She says we have parties there. If you are especially intrigued by this level of experience and inter lifetime please read what Sylvia and Francine have to say.

It is wrong of me to refer to any human here as deceased. We are beyond our previous life when we are in inter lifetime. We are beyond healing and assimilation of the prior life. Humans are here to learn and experience. Humans here can also be planning for their next incarnation. Humans here can be delaying ascension while they help others here and on earth.

Inter lifetime is a long phase of experience. It is much, much longer than our time on earth. Every human has been through the human species consciousness pool to plan this lifetime on their way to the earth. So why don't we remember this place? Maybe in order to have free will to make choices we need to forget the reason we picked our family and the plans we made before this life. I don't know why we cannot remember our pre-birth experiences but I hope to find that out one day. I could spend a lot of my meditation time exploring the human species consciousness pool, but why take time in life to do this? We all have this marvelous place to look forward to.

THE HOLY SPIRIT

Chapter Twelve

Ascension

God is the point of origin
and the point of all return.
Eventually when we complete our
God-given intent, we return to God.

Home is one of the most compelling words we humans have. It represents comfort, security, familiarity, peacefulness and relaxation. Home is a place where we can be ourselves. In our work-a-day world, home is what we have to leave and look forward to returning to. Our original home was in God/Source. In some part of each of us we know God/Source is our true home, the one we are trying to find our way back to.

Ascension is the journey back home to God/Source. It is the heaven our religions speak about. Ascension is being enfolded, for what we would think of as eternities, in goodness, in beauty, in light, in the most positive energy expressions of God/Source. In ascension, we are completely outside of any relationship to time and we are released from the potential limitations of physical existence. Ascension is eons and eons of merging with other life forms also ascending. Ultimately our souls, the part of our self with which we intercept and pass on the divine, merge totally into God/Source.

The journey out from God/Source was the process of separation. In order to know ourselves as individuals we followed a path of separation culminating in life on earth. In life we know ourselves as something divided from other people, other species. We feel loneliness because of this separation. We can seem very far from God/Source here on earth.

The journey back to God/Source is a process of unification. We retain our self knowing ability during ascension. However, our selfhood becomes less and less important to us as we unite our energy with others. When we are completely merged with God/Source, ultimately, we cease to know our self as an individual, as a species, as an ego, as anything separate from God/Source. This is the true end of our journey.

Ascension is the exit door out of the circle of life. The choice for ascension is the choice to leave these levels of physical experience forever. We will not reincarnate after this choice is enacted. Ascension is not inter lifetime. The deceased are outside of or beyond the possibility to choose reincarnation into physical manifestation on earth after ascension is initiated.

The beginning of the journey of ascension can start from any level of the afterlife. Keep in mind that the near-earth deceased experience, the completion of individual work and complete healing from the prior life can happen in an instant. Ascension can begin shortly after physical death in terms of earth time, or an individual may not choose to begin their ascension for ages.

I have met many people in life with ascending attitudes. These people are not necessary religious although many are. Some common attributes are they live and breathe in the love of God and their deeply internal goal is to enact God's will in whatever way they understand it. Ascending people abide by the spiritual laws, which include self responsibility and the golden rule. They know there is a price for everything and there is an effort required to complete their God given intent is a balance of action and prayer. Ascending people also emit a glow of love that impacts people they meet. I have only been able to contact one deceased individual who was in the early stages of ascension. I was particularly interested in contacting Jean as she was an incredible, powerfully spiritual person in life. I knew if

I could find her, and she was willing to communicate, that I would learn from her.

In meditation I had the sensation of traveling a great distance. The word firmament came to mind as I seemed to be at the outer edge of the universe, and I was traveling even beyond that and going deeper into a trance state. I kept traveling leaving starlight and into a blackness or blankness. Then I reached what seemed to be a huge gravitational field. The gravitational force was coming from an immense light, and even though the light is a very long way away I felt its influence on my mental vehicle. I asked again to go to a place where I can reach Jean.

Then I had the idea of bands of color that were spread out around the far off light. My mental vehicle was smaller than a fraction of a speck of dust here, and I feel like I am on an odyssey. I entered a pink/mauve band of energy. I perceived a sphere close to me, transparent like a crystal ball. Then like two drops of water running together and merging on a window I found myself inside this sphere. I realized I was not going to get a clear representation of Jean but I trusted and felt I had reached her essence.

I went ahead and asked what is the importance of religious practice in our life. The following information comes: God is the beginning and the end, God is the point of origin and the point of all return. God is the source of light and life and of all manifestation. Religion is the expression of this truth. People who are religious will reincarnate in the knowledge of this truth, at least that is how it was for Jean. The church was as close as she could get to God in life, she felt God there. When we pray we know we are expressions of God. To pray for someone else is to acknowledge that they are an expression of God.

I then had more of a sense that Jean was speaking to me. Jean said when her sister died, they got together immediately and had their playtime. In the near-earth deceased experience they said their farewells to life. They visited the great cathedrals. They didn't have to stop or stay at the hub city. Jean's and her sister's individual work took place in a flash. But Jean did spend more time here (I think she means near the earth) than she wanted to waiting for her sister. She says they are together in ascension and are much more just beings than humans now. She is also combined (or commingled) with others of the same essence.

Jean's thoughts continued. Our time in life is like a glint of light on one snowflake. Our time in life is infinitesimal compared to the existence of our being. All of your lifetimes over centuries and centuries are but a split second in relationship to the whole of the journey.

I asked then, why experience life, why do we get caught up in the small details of our physical life? She answered: everything can be a metaphor for God. Everything in life can be experienced in that context. All the potential of God have to be expressed. All the potentials of the potentials have to be expressed and we participate in the flowering of God's expression. You should be content in your present because you will find your way back to God. After she said this, I could not keep my focus so I mentally returned to my body.

A deceased individual may delay ascension by prolonging experience in any of the levels of the afterlife. The ascending deceased may wait near the earth for a beloved one to die in order to act as a greeter or guide.

They may cross the earth portal and wait in any level of the plane of conceptualized heavens/realities, or may go on to wait at the city of light. There they will project a thought construction to inhabit and even take up meaningful activities to help others while delaying ascension. The reason most ascending deceased choose to remain within the potential of physical life and delay ascension is that they are waiting for others to complete their life purpose so they may ascend together.

While the decision to enact ascension can be made at any point in the afterlife, the choice to ascend is made in life. It is not as if we stand on the threshold of choice and the thought of ascension dawns on us. The deceased who choose ascension have had ascension as their goal all through life, normally through many lifetimes. The desire to ascend has shone as a deep personal beacon with which they have charted the course of their lives.

There are characteristics that people with an ascending orientation share in life. They know what a gift time in life is and treasure it. They are detached from material possessions, the allure of wealth, even if they possess material wealth. Along with this detachment, ironically, they have a refined sense of appreciation for life. They celebrate what is beauty, truth and love in life. Ascending people are loving people so they can't help but be engaged with other people and life forms.

This love of life, yet a certain detachment from life, is expressed beautifully in this quote by William Wilberford (1759-1833). He wrote: "I now feel so weaned from the earth, my affections so much in Heaven, that I can leave you all without regret, yet I do not love you less, but God more."

The activities that lead us to the knowledge of ascension can be summed up in this short phrase, "the striving for excellence." We express God/Source by trying to be the best we can at any given task in life. There are ascension-oriented people who are recognized as special humans, for example, Ghandi, Mother Theresa, Anwar Sadat, Socrates, Buckminster Fuller or Jimmy Carter to name a very few. We may not know about, say, someone who has worked their whole life to save a species or subspecies of a plant or animal. The people who adopt or foster children in order to protect and nurture them are not famous in our media. Millions of people with ascending orientations exist dedicated to excellence in life that are never famous.

People may be excellent in any small activity of life, for example, being a kind and generous maintenance worker in an apartment building, or a skilled nurse, or a dedicated teacher. People striving for excellence in sports can be trying to learn of ascension. Musicians and artists expressing beauty through their music can be energizing their choice for ascension. The striving for, not necessarily the achieving of, excellence in at least one of life's activities will eventually awaken in us our memory of God/Source, our memory of home.

When we came out of God/Source we all carried something of God/Source to express. We carried our intent, what we would attempt to express as a human on earth. Before the choice of ascension is enacted people have a sense they have fulfilled or completed their God given intent. This intent is commonly expressed over many lifetimes before a deep inner sense of completion is reached.

The conscious desire to ascend while we are in life, coupled with a surety that we have expressed our God given intent is what precedes the choice for ascension. A very few people ascend after one lifetime. These people spent ages before life planning and learning how to complete their intent. Most of us practice being as good as we can lifetime after lifetime. It really doesn't matter how long it takes to learn of ascension and energize that choice. But as ascending becomes a more and more compelling focus on a deeply personal level, life becomes a continual prayer. The constant orientation toward God/Source, beauty, light, unity keeps exercising and reinforcing the choice for ascension.

Ascension is an individual conscious choice. Only the individual can gauge for themselves if they have completed their intended expression of God/Source. Ask yourself, is there one thing you would regret not having done before you die? Keep asking yourself that question and it may give hints about what your intent in life is.

Once I was told, in meditation, that the intent I came from God/Source with is simply bridging a gap. I know I have had several lifetimes on earth. Several lifetimes when I wasn't doing my intent work, several lifetimes that I struggled in ignorance, made mistakes, and was more involved in the people near me than I was in my spiritual evolution. In this lifetime I have gotten derailed from working on the completion of my intent. On one hand I am looking forward to going home to God/Source and on the other I feel a sadness about irrevocably leaving the earth and all its beauty.

Our organized religions teach the truth of ascension. Religions can supply the tools to learn of ascension but they cannot supply the motivation that comes from within each individual. We cannot assume that because someone has a religious life that they have completed their intent and have energized their choice for ascension sufficiently in this lifetime. Of course there are religious people who are at this juncture in their personal evolution and through their example, helping others awaken their inner pursuit of ascension. Other religious people may still be working at understanding ascension for themselves. We cannot earn ascension through good works alone, or religious practices alone. Ascension is not earned. Ascension is learned.

Even people who never have any religious affiliation or pursue any of the religious metaphors that teach this truth can learn of ascension. Anyone living with any sense of fairness or justice toward themselves, to their fellow man, and to the other creatures on the planet will ultimately learn of ascension. It is a goal most every human will achieve for themselves, no matter how long it takes to find the key.

We can't just decide that we want out of the experience of physical life and choose to ascend. That is not enough. Even if we understand what ascension is, the single-minded choice for ascension is normally carried throughout and reinforced by actions in many sequential lifetimes. Ascension has to become the goal in every fiber of our body, mind and spirit.

People can, however, destroy their own possibility for ever learning of the choice of ascension by participating in repeated acts of evil and destructiveness in life. This self imposed exile from God/Source is the hell that religions speak of. We will look at this in the following chapter. Unless great malignant acts of evil are enacted repeatedly in life and redemption from those actions is never sought, ascension can be learned of, eventually, by everyone.

I had a lot of questions about activities in life that foster the knowledge and the choice for ascension. Who better to ask than Joseph Campbell, the esteemed mythologist. This is a transcript of a meditation done in August 1988, shortly after Joseph had died.

After dedicating myself to good and for God, I asked to be with Joseph Campbell. I followed a path to the visualization of a house. This house has sliding glass doors that face the ocean. There is also a kind and gracious woman here. We greet each other and she leaves us for our talk. I am sitting on an oatmeal colored couch and Joe is sitting to my right. I comment on how nice it is that you two are staying together. He replies, "when you know things are possible you can create them for yourself."

I said to Joe, We were both brought up in the Catholic church. Praying for the dead was a part of every Mass. Even prayers for the deceased you did not know were offered up. But there was also so much barter of prayers for sins, so much black and white. How did you relate to the church?"

He answered, "It was the ritual of the Latin Mass that took away the language that we knew. When we participated in the ritual of the old Latin Mass, we would be transported out of our life. Everything was different from our everyday life. The interior of the church was a unique building, with the high ceilings and stained glass windows. It was a quiet place, the incense even made it smell different. The church had a feeling of being isolated from the rest of the world. All these things forced you to a place in your mind where you didn't see anything you ordinarily saw, you didn't feel, sense, or hear anything in your ordinary life. You could experience the transcendent nature of yourself away from your common everyday experience. We were transported by the ritual, very much like you are transported when you meditate."

"Remember the tabernacle. It was a very mysterious thing on the altar. It was covered and when the cover was removed it was shining gold. And even when the door of the tabernacle was opened there was a veil across the opening. The priest reached behind the veil to bring out the ciborium, (a gold chalice-like cup). What he brought out was a symbol of the mystery that is God. The tabernacle was the point of power in the church, more so than the Crucifix. The tabernacle was the symbolic source of the Holy Spirit, and that was a powerful concept."

"I think it all fell apart when they tried to bring the everyday world into the Mass. Celebrants and servers, readers and musicians began to come and go during Mass. In the older tradition, the doors were closed during Mass. The only movements were quiet and restrained."

"The styles of the churches also changed. Some were more open, more public and less special. It was not like taking a journey to another place anymore, an isolated place so different from anywhere else in our life. The churches became like shopping malls, with multiple openings and exits, bringing the outside world in. These things just diminished the ritual's ability to transport people's consciousness to a higher level of experience."

"What still happens in church, in any church, is a group dynamic. When people join in prayer they can generate the feeling of transcendence and share it. This happens more readily in the Baptist churches through song and movement. An effective priest or preacher can create the feeling of transcendence with words that will evoke a particular mind set that can be powerfully felt throughout the congregation."

I said to Joe that here in New England the older smaller churches are still used. The traditional architecture is still a beautiful environment to celebrate the mystery of the Word made flesh. I find the funeral Mass a particularly moving ritual, even if it is in English. But as a child I experienced profound rapture out in nature more often than in church. I felt as if I was exactly the same energy as the trees, the birds and the wind, and I was completely in my present. It has always bothered me that we are taught we cannot experience the part of us that is divine without following the codes of any particular religion. Joe answered, "you have to allow yourself to experience the divine. It is possible in any walking waking moment in your life."

"Your experience of divinity is not dependent on going somewhere or following certain rules. Experiencing divinity within yourself is not dependent on doing anything that anyone else may do. You can achieve rapture anywhere. What is so difficult is when someone meets someone who has achieved rapture, then you want to follow their rules. You want to do exactly as they did, whether it is going to the top of a mountain and fasting, or being locked in a dungeon for forty days."

"People who achieved rapture are spiritual people who are walking in the knowledge of their divinity. Other people see this and there tends to be a following to recreate the circumstances that are believed to have caused the rapture. Practices are mimicked, rules are constructed, not by the saintly people but by the followers."

"Sometimes it is helpful to look at how another person has achieved transcendence, rapture, or the feeling of the divine connection they have with God/Source. Study or the following of religious practices will help a person find their own path to the awareness of their own divinity. Finding this awareness of the soul or spirit becomes harder when more complexity surrounds your life. The more distracted you are the more you have to work on focusing on the activities that produce and foster rapture within yourself."

"I found a lot to be rapturous about in the human mind. I am stimulated by what others have written and felt. For example, for me to meet someone who is able to converse with the deceased fascinates me. Your mind fires me up, I find this very interesting. I see divinity in that. But this is not your path to divinity. Your path is through the natural elements. Your transcendence comes from your experience in the texture, the smells and the reality of the earth."

"I see divinity in exceptional people. Yes, I focused mostly on people in my life, but on people striving to be excellent as many native people are. They did not get distracted or weighed down by the complexity of the modern world. Practicing excellence puts you in touch with your own divine nature. Being the best that you can be will always break down the barriers to the understanding and the knowledge of your own divinity."

I asked Joe how he related to God. He answered, "I found God everywhere I looked. Once you tune into what is divine, there is so much divinity here that you never have to look beyond the planet itself. There is divinity in the most simple person trying to be the best that they can. There is divinity in the sacrifice of motherhood, in the giving over of your life to a complete and separate other life (the child). There is divinity in the father, the nurturer, the provider, the protector, if this is done with excellence. The quest for the Holy Grail was all about striving for excellence."

"This concept is throughout myths and literature. It's not necessarily in the achieving of the act, the end of a chosen act, because in the striving for excellence, the excellence exists. The excellence is not diminished by whether or not we succeed or complete the task. It is in the striving, the trying, the exercising of yourself to your highest capacity that is the achievement, the excellence, the divinity in you."

"The word excel is so closely related to the word excellence. Too often we see in societies the reward system of money as the only gauge of excellence. No matter what the end, excellence is in the trying to express excellence. To not try equals waste, and waste is evil. Time is an energy we must strive not to waste. This doesn't mean we are just hamsters on a wheel in a cage, just running and running. Excellence can be achieved in pure pleasure, if you are sitting and resting, taking pleasure in your rest. Being completely in your present is an expression of excellence."

I asked Joe about prayer and its function in our life. He answered, "if you stand on a rock near the ocean watching the light on the water and are completely where you are in your present, that is prayer. It is the achieving of eternity. Eternity has nothing to do with time. Eternity is a state of being. Many people achieve this

185

transcendence through certain verbal patterns that we all agree on as prayer. An example of this is people who pray with a rosary. The rosary is a ritual."

"Ritualistic prayers are a trigger to achieve certain states, like the psalms for example. They work for some people and not others. You are the type that can achieve eternity by experiencing the wind, the sunshine and the sounds of nature. To others, nature is an alien concept, and would hardly help them achieve transcendence. They would worry about the bugs. Here in the afterlife, I experience divinity by turning my thoughts toward God/Source. The Source of all radiance, the Source of all of us, everything that exists."

"I could ascend now. I could focus on the radiance and will myself to be in complete unity with it. This would be the losing of myself in the sense that some religions speak of. It is not just the loss of ego, not just the loss of earthly concerns, the loss of vanity, but the complete loss of self knowledge. When one is merged with God/Source it is the complete loss of the self. The garden of Eden, original sin was the knowledge of our separation from God/Source. When one is merged with God/Source there is no separation possible. But, there is more I want to do within the human experience."

"I had a great life. I was not handicapped. My parents were kind and treated me with love. Believe me, there were a lot of days when I got up, went and did my teaching, came home, had a drink and dinner and went to bed. I had many dark days, not every day was in the light, not every day was lived in excellence. Sometimes life was just too much effort, and then I just let the days go by until I was recharged, the weather changed, I had a vacation, or something encouraged me. But I tried more than I did not try."

"On the one hand I had my everyday activities, bringing as much excellence as I could into whatever I was doing. On the other hand I practiced simply being in the eternal, the present. Life is a combination of these two. Certainly life, in a practical sense is action. It is not just about transcendence. It is about doing the best you can and also just being."

"There are no rules, except the physical laws that we live in. To experience divinity there are no rules for how to do it. Each of us has the power to experience the divine by ourselves. When you are praying just try to be there in the moment, try to experience the eternal a little bit, try to be empty, calm and just be. We don't need to follow any rules or anyone else's path to achieve transcendence. Be as excellent as you can in whatever constructive activity you choose to do and acknowledge that within yourself that is divine, the core of God/Source within all of us." I thanked Joe for his beautiful words and returned to my body.

Ascending deceased have known they were, at their core, soul or spirit in life, so self realization after death is already in place. They know how to achieve self healing after death in a split second because they have been energizing themselves through prayer all their life. Ascending deceased can progress very quickly through the after death processes. They may or may not choose to spend much time near the earth after they die. The earth portal is a necessary transition but assimilation of the prior life can take place in a blink. These deceased can choose to by-pass the human species consciousness pool because there is no more work to accomplish there. The ascending deceased are well familiar with all the processes and stages of the afterlife because they most likely have been through these experiences before.

The ascending deceased still pass across the threshold of choice to exit the potential of physical life. This transition can seem like yet another death. The first transition is the physical death, the second is the earth portal, the third at the threshold of choice and then ascension is the final and irreversible transition out of the cycle of physical life. It is a big step, a big decision, but this choice has been made and energized long before physical death. The choice to ascend is a great, glorious and wondrous choice. But then, so is being in life.

I believe there are many realms of experience, beyond the circle of life, in which individuals can manifest and continue to express a God/Source given intent. When we leave the circle of life in ascension it may not preclude more expression of our individual energy in some other arena or forum.

We may, even within the journey of ascension, be able to have other phases of expression in energy levels that we can't comprehend with our physical human mind. As we purify our individual self knowing energy it makes sense that we would have an even larger array of experiences available to participate in. This is what we may find out when the time comes, that our journey and expansion may continue outside of this circle of life. When we have the choice for ascension it may also give us other glorious opportunities for the expression of our God/Source intent. No matter what comes after ascension I believe it will be in the light, be in the goodness of God's love.

Chapter Thirteen

The Descended Deceased

Our advance or descent is created
by our chosen actions in life.
What we do in life can set the stage
for our eternity.

As I write this chapter on a March morning I am glancing out at the frozen river across the road from our house. Water started flowing over the ice a few days ago. When the ice breaks up or goes out, it sounds like a freight train. The ice gathers, jams, that jam breaks and moves down and more jams come down from further up the river. The ice can come up over the banks and block the road. Some people find this natural event violent and frightening. I always hope the ice breaks in the daytime so I can watch it. Some years there are huge vertically held pieces of ice that look like whales moving downstream. This is a powerful and majestic thing to see, at least it is to me. People here choose to think differently about this shared event. As individuals we make choices all the time about what we see and think.

Everyone's experience of life is so different. Take, for example, what we choose to view in our media. The ugly, the negative side of human experience is presented in the media. So is knowledge. One person may have a natural reluctance to watch or read about the negative possibilities or activities in life. Others delight in the ugly, the pornographic, the nasty, or the violence portrayed in the media.

Certainly, the majority of people on earth are simply trying to live the best they can. We aren't all missionaries, or spending our lives working in soup kitchens. Most of us try to accomplish our goals of caring for ourselves and our family, our property and the part of the world we live in. This is the norm. We coexist, we participate in physical existence, we meet our needs and simply live as best we can. We don't steal from others or set about to harm others.

Nonetheless, all people have the capacity to create both positively and negatively. Examples of positive creation are deliberately loving our self, our friends and family, kindness to others, learning, striving to improve at any goal or task, life affirming actions, fulfilling our spiritual path. Negative creation would be actions destructive to the self or others, such as wasting of time or life and destroying what is within our influence. We seem to be the only species on earth that is participating in this dance of opposites. Some, in the new age movement, deny the existence of evil, calling it ignorance, and in one sense it is ignorance. Others say evil does not exist, that this is a virtual world -like a dream so nothing - not even evil, is real here. I couldn't disagree more. Our life may be a tiny part in our evolution as an individual but it is vitally important that we achieve self realization and purify our soul as much as possible in life.

Evil is the destruction of energy; the destruction of an energy form. The potential for the destruction of energy came from God/Source as well as the potential for energy gain. It has to go both ways, that is just the way it is. If energy can be saved, retrieved and enhanced then energy also has to be able to be lost. When God/Source sends energy forth some simply will not return, multiply, or be enhanced. Some will be wasted or lost.

The way our negative creations impact our life is similar to how they may impact our afterlife. Physical life is a sensual experience, driven by the need for food, for warmth and comfort, the animal needs we have because we are in a physical body. The sensual comfort of a full belly is universal, no matter what the animal species. The need for touch is also universal, whether it is plants reaching toward each other, or young animals nesting with their mother. The need for play, physical activity and movement is universal. Perhaps this is so even with trees when they sway in the wind. Seeing the colors of our world is a sensual experience no matter how we, any animal or insect perceives sunlight or moonlight. Because of our physical bodies, we enjoy sensual experience here. There is certainly nothing wrong with this. It is simply where I must start to explain that different levels of experience exist even within physical life.

A less energized, or lower experience of life can be described as insatiable needs. A person may be caught up in self destructive addictive desires, even if the basic physical needs of food, comfort, warmth, or shelter are met. Life, for these people, is not bright, not happy. Colors are not enjoyed. Beauty and goodness are not perceived, are not sought out.

I always think of this level of physical experience as being forever in artificial light. This is the life experience of never having enough, never being grateful for even the smallest of comforts. Life is lived as a drone, where work is misery and helping others does not cross our mind. We are too caught up in our own insatiable needs to care. This can be considered a level of the underworld that exists parallel and within our normal physical experience. It is the dwelling level of people ensnared in self destructive, life threatening patterns of addiction.

An even lower or less energized experience in life can be summed up in one word: pain. Life is dark, sharp and filled with pain- whether mental, physical, spiritual or any combination. For these people the feeling of being in physical is all negative. Pain obliterates even the desire for satiation, pain itself is the reality. Emotions of despair are chronic. People living among us are in this level of experience.

Many of us experience physical pain from time to time in life. Even people in chronic pain can adopt an attitude of making the best of it. They find some small thing for which to be grateful. The circumstances of this lower level of experience includes, however, a lack of empathy with or caring for others. People in this level of the underworld do not exercise the ability to love. They do not have any spiritual pursuits, and do not strive to make the best of the condition they are in.

I am trying to illustrate that even within life there are gradients or levels of experience. These gradients of experience are all around us as we participate in life. We constantly make choices which form our lifetime experience. I think of physical life experience from the highest expression of humanness to the lowest as living in joy, happiness, gratitude, curiosity, comfort, dissatisfaction, depression, pain or numbness. This is important to our deceased experience because when someone dies they initially continue within the same aspects of experience they participated in on earth.

An even lower level of life expression than insatiable desires or pain exists. Some people deliberately choose to descend in life. They choose to express the dark, the neurotic, the dangerous and the evil side of human nature. They pursue a life dedicated to destruction and evil. They harm themselves, they harm who and what they can. They waste the opportunity of physical life with repetitive destructive acts.

Self-destructiveness is a key factor to an evil life. Someone who cares nothing for themselves will care nothing for anyone else. Evil is a deeply internal choice that begins with number one: the self. The conscious intent to express evil should not be confused with a self destructive mental illness. Evil people are extremely conscious and deliberate in their actions.

The attitudes that we have in life continue to be our attitudes in the afterlife. Someone who dies after a lifetime devoted to evil will continue in that orientation after death. Things don't change for them much, except that the expression of evil, the ability to destroy, is not available. They may still have the will to destroy in their mind but they are powerless to affect any experience other than their own.

These deceased are debilitated by self-induced ignorance after death and are unable to progress in a normal and natural way through the after death processes of self realization, assimilation and healing. They have depleted themselves to such a place of ignorance that they have little innate knowledge or common sense with which to function in the afterlife. They have no interest in those who repeatedly come to help them. They are also uninterested in building any more knowledge for themselves. They have created a deeply internal ignorant state for themselves.

These descended deceased remain in the underworld after death. They remain on the same lightless level of pain or insatiable needs they participated in on earth. A long time ago, a psychic said to me, "Hitler is a rock". I understand now he was saying that whatever is left of Hitler is trapped in the inert or lowest possible energy level of the afterlife.

Some descended deceased don't know there are any options for them because of their ignorance. These deceased may not even see the earth portal, or if they do they won't understand it. They have not fostered love, so the greeters in the near-earth deceased experience may either be ignored or their attempt to influence the descended deceased toward love and light may be scorned.

These deceased may mentally continue the same patterns of habitual destructiveness in which they participated when alive. These deceased would not understand that they can change their age or move around very much on earth. They may make it from the hospital or the nursing home to their favorite bar, but they won't explore the beauty of the Grand Canyon, for example. They would stay where they were because their knowledge is reduced to only what is familiar.

Because these deceased stay where they had lived, there can be a build-up of the descended deceased in wretched areas of cities. As a result, a metaphysical pollution of these disembodied people exist that some of us are sensitive enough to feel. I remember when the only road to Providence, Rhode Island went through a seedy, industrial area where there were train tracks and a lot of bars. I always hated to drive through there. Perhaps I was sensing all the descended deceased hanging around those bars. It is no wonder that bars are also sometimes called "haunts".

This crush of earth-bound spirits continues to increase. Crimes and war increase with increasing populations on earth. As the destructive orientation increases with populations, more and more descended deceased have entrapped themselves here. The planet cannot shrug off this pollution.

When all of the universe returns to God/Source everything that exists will return, including these descended deceased in whatever state of self knowing they may be abiding. We cannot conceive of the physical universe returning to God/Source in a time reference we can grasp. Ultimately there will be an end of them and whatever level of pain they have created for themselves.

Evil deceased are drawn to evil people in life. The descended deceased cannot participate in destruction the way they did in life. But they can observe it in others here. They remain near people committing the same addictions or perversion they were fixated on in life. They will stay near the living, participating in whatever evil they were obsessed with in life, whether it is drug addiction, murder, sexual abuse or violence. Degraded people in life tend to get a following of these deceased who have entrapped themselves in this low level of the afterlife. The descended deceased do not know of anything else to do.

Spirit possession and parasitic bonding of the descended deceased with the living is limited to these lower levels of life. It is common for people in descending activities in life to simply be followed and observed by like-minded deceased than actually possessed by them. Anyone living a normal, sane life has an energy shield in place around them because of the way we are energized by simply being alive.

The barrier that divides the living from the deceased is impenetrable for the greatest majority of us. The health and vitality of this barrier can be eroded by self-destructive acts of excessive drug and alcohol use combined with a personal orientation toward negative neurosis and evil. A profound negative openness in the living is necessary to admit the influence of a descended deceased into the living's energy field. The descended deceased have limited energy to begin with and without knowing how to draw in energy they become depleted and weaker.

It is interesting that the intent to commit evil in life can be brought into life with the pre-birth focus. Remember that at the human species consciousness pool, all of human experience is available to be explored. This includes the descending or negative, destructive activities of humans as well. A personality can study evil in inter lifetime. This helps explain the nature versus nurture aspect when we may know of a child born to parents who are sensible, knowledgeable and even spiritual. This child's needs may be met, and the parenting of this child may include the same sacrifice and love that any parent's care of a child entails. Yet this child will bring with him or her the fascination with and appeal for evil and will choose to enact evil.

The opposite can be true, where a child is born to parents who are already degraded through self destructive and evil participation, yet this child has enough innate knowledge to express his or her humanness on earth in a positive way. For this child to even simply learn to work, support itself in adulthood, and take care of the basics of life is a profound accomplishment. Some of these children become great teachers and helpers here. The intention we bring into life can overcome the circumstances we find ourselves born into.

Of course we can be influenced in a positive or negative way by the people around us in life. When someone is a victim of tremendous violence and evil, there is a risk that they will take this violence and evil into themselves. They may then proceed in life in ignorance and descent. However, if they die as a result of the violence, they can be helped by people praying for them. If they are open to it, legions of helpers exist that are coming from higher energy states dedicated to soul rescue.

Saving a soul's energy happens the same way it does on earth when a truly good person can try to effect a change toward good and toward God/Source with another living individual. The choice to ultimately change an orientation from descent to ascent cannot happen unless a personality is open to change, unless they realize and want to change for themself, whether in life or after life. At the moment of death, a personality who has led a descending life can have an epiphany, and turn back toward the light. This is the redemption of which our religions speak.

I debated with myself whether to include this material in Choices In the Afterlife. For one thing, the greatest majority of deceased function beautifully when they die. No one reading this book will be dedicated to evil in life. Simply the act of seeking knowledge is an ascending choice. I decided to include it because if I didn't it would leave out a piece of the puzzle. Also, it is important in life to understand that we create at least the beginning of the reality in our afterlife.

The meditation I have chosen to end this chapter was one of the earliest ones I was asked to do by a living friend. At the time I thought Leo was trapped in his own belief of a lightless void. He was stuck alright in a place we can think of as the underworld.

When I opened in meditation I saw a figure to the left of me whose body and clothing were devoid of color, like a black and white television. I threw white light over this figure and the shape of him became more distinct. He said his name was Leo, which was his astrological sign in life. He did not want to tell me his name. I asked to be closer to Leo so we could talk.

I moved to a gray spiral. I had the feeling of winding inward in this dark gray-blue spiral. I finally got to what seemed to be the bottom, or the far end. I was standing with Leo. I asked Leo why he was staying at such an un-energized place. He said he didn't know what else to do. I suggested we go back to the moment of his death.

He then showed me an explosion and his upper body flying apart. For a second I thought it was a car accident but he showed me that he shot himself in his bedroom. He said, "it was like I blew my spirit to bits along with my body. My mind was disintegrated. I was so blasted apart I was not aware of the funeral, the people, the mess or any of it." I asked if he saw the light or any other people when he died. He said, "the bottom part of me that was more intact did move toward the light, but I was more a mass than a person right then. I have just been in this gray-blue limbo ever since."

I asked Leo if he could remember when he knew he was dead. He said, "I believed death would be the end of me. That is why I committed suicide. I experienced the destruction of myself. But gradually, bit by bit, the pieces of myself attracted each other and re-formed into myself. The pieces of myself (his memory body) just gravitated together. This was not an act of will on my part. After I was put back together I didn't relate to myself as being dead, I thought of myself as being reassembled. But even now that I am reassembled I feel like I have lost my direction, lost my plan or code to follow."

I then asked Leo if he would like to be in the light, if I could try to move him out of this dark place. He said, "sure what have I got to lose?" I surrounded Leo with the white light of God's love and reached out to hold him. He was crying on my shoulder, saying he never realized how much his death would hurt his family. He said he did not want to look around or see anything because he did not want to realize how much he had hurt them.

I visualized us climbing out of the gray spiral. I held him as we came out of the spiral and came into a brighter place. Leo said he did not feel worthy of this place. I told him he had no choice but to stay here. I visualized colors, and healing energy around Leo. I saw some of it sticking to him; he became less gray.

I took a while to talk to Leo about prayer. I told him he is going to have to find the will within himself to heal and forgive himself. I visualized an iridescent disk for him to use as a platform and told him I would pray for him.

But Leo just kept going over and over his death. I said to Leo, "I know your death was a profound experience but the forces of love are powerful, you can get healed of it." What seemed odd to me was Leo seemed attracted to the gray-blue spiral we came out of. I moved to stand between Leo and the darkness. I urged him to stay in the light to seek self healing.

I asked him about his childhood and he wasn't very open about it. I asked Leo if he could remember a time in his life when he was happy. I took some time then to explain the continuity between life and the afterlife. I told him there is no judgment, but there is a reason for our individual existence. I then helped him with some visualizations based on his memories to keep him in the color and told him I would be back to check on him.

A few months later, in meditation, I asked to go where Leo was. Immediately I was greeted by a blue-eyed, blond young man who seemed about sixteen years old. He is wearing a blue chambray shirt, jeans and deck shoes. He had a narrow face with good bone definition and regular features. We shook hands and I sat on his platform facing him.

Leo said, "I am starting to feel better about myself. I have started to move around. I have started to think about the hard things, how much I hurt my whole family, how much I hurt myself. Watching them and being near them is hard. But this is better than being stuck where I was."

In this meditation I realized Leo was still in one of the lower levels of the near-earth deceased experience. I had accessed healing energy for him but he hadn't yet progressed up any of the levels of the deceased experience. I explained he could take all the time he wanted to be near the earth and eventually he would have the focus and the will to move on. I spent more time with Leo talking over what he could learn from his brief life and about how precious the gift of time in life is. I told him I would keep him in my prayers. At least Leo was in his present, a point at which he could assimilate his experience in life and his suicide, heal enough and eventually move on.

The evolution of our personality and completion of intent takes place over several lifetimes. Although it is possible to complete one's God-given intent in one lifetime, it is rare. The great majority of us cement the course for our personality in the manifesting level, which for us is life on earth. It is within life that continuance of our personality in the afterlife is formed and developed. It is essential that we use our short time in life well. Our advances and our descents, our choices in life echo through eternity.

Chapter Fourteen

Soul Rescue

There is always help for those who seek it.

The best book I have ever read on the afterlife is What Dreams May Come, by Richard Matheson (Tor Press, 1998, New York, copyright 1978, Richard Matheson). It is a love story. I found our copy in the romance section of a bookstore. The book was made into a movie and won an Academy Award for best visual effects in 1988. Both the book and the movie are powerful works of art.

I agree with every line in the book and the movie based on my research and work with the deceased. What Dreams May Come is the story of one soul rescuing another. A woman's children are killed in an auto accident. Later, her husband dies and she is so distraught that she kills herself. After her suicide, she is a ghost trapped in a colorless, emotionally painful underworld level of the near-earth deceased experience. The deceased husband's love is so great that he is determined to save her soul even at the risk of being ensnared in her reality with her.

Soul rescue is helping or positively influencing a deceased person toward self realization and the healing necessary for them to assimilate their life and death and progress in the afterlife. Soul rescue was the early focus of my private psychic work. In meditation I would reach and try to help selected deceased from my present point of power to their present, if they were conscious. We can all do some of the work of soul rescue when we pray for the deceased and remember them with love.

There are deceased who are not in the light or are not functioning well through no fault of their own. People who die in a sudden accident or who are murdered may or may not be doing well in the afterlife.

Emotions of fear or anger, generated by the manner of the death, can be carried in the mind of the deceased and inhibit their consciousness for a while. This self generated fear and anger may so completely overwhelm the deceased that they are unable to clearly see their way to self realization. Until they reach self realization, they cannot begin to function in the afterlife. These people especially need our prayers and remembering. They are inhibited from not only consciousness, but from the ability to energize themselves through a positive outlook or attitude.

Self induced mental disabilities, such as drug abuse, can also impair consciousness after death. I do not find this the case with degenerative diseases such as Alzheimers or the senility common in the elderly. These deceased have known themselves at some point in their lives and when the damaged brain is dropped at death, the mind will function clearly. I believe any disoriented deceased can be helped or guided in order to move on. Remember there are many deceased in inter lifetime, ∤as well as other higher beings who have never been in life, dedicated to soul rescue.

I have a particular compassion for people who commit suicide. Yes, suicide is a chosen self-destructive act and most of the time is not a positive choice for the personality. But I also feel that people who commit suicide are victims of depression, or despair. There was a time in my life when I thought nothing could ever change, that things would never get better and the only way out was through suicide. I think that experience was to teach me the compassion I would draw on when working with people who enact suicide. I have committed suicide in a previous lifetime. I deeply understand how thoughts of despair can take over the mind.

I feel the friends and families of suicide victims are conflicted by guilt, anger, or rejection. With these ranges of emotions, there are not as many people praying for and loving suicide victims as there are for deceased who are victims of heart attacks, car accidents or murders. Suicide victims often do not have the clear, loving energy coming to them from the living which so greatly benefits the deceased.

People who commit suicide believe suicide will make things better. They believe they will be out of their emotional pain. However, their mental pain is carried in their mind into the deceased state. Deceased by suicide usually believe they will be annihilated through the act of suicide. They are dismayed when they realize this is not true.

The act of suicide is not always a wrong choice. I have worked with several suicides who were terminally ill, who couldn't bear the physical pain. Suicide in the extreme elderly is becoming more common. It is always sad for those of us left behind. Nevertheless, many of these deceased achieved self realization easily after death, and had started to heal and assimilate their life.

More often than not, suicide in early or mid life is a set back to the personal evolution of the deceased. They will have to work toward the learning that will prevent this act from being chosen in another lifetime. But all suicides can achieve self realization and progress after death. Most suicides do have to work at finding (or remembering) something positive in their life to focus on in order to achieve self realization and progress.

This is where humans from every level, doing the work of soul rescue, come in. If the deceased who committed suicide are open to communication, I can help them find at least one positive memory from life. I then urge these deceased to dwell on or in that memory. With effort, this positive thought can replace negative ones in the mind of the deceased. The more positive memories the deceased concentrate on, the better able they are to move toward healing and into more energized levels of the afterlife. I act as a coach so they can create a more positive mental outlook and begin to forgive themselves for their suicide.

I would like to close this chapter with Camilla's story. Camilla's death was not a suicide, but my work with Camilla was one of the more complex acts of soul rescue in which I have ever been involved. Camilla died in a car accident. In the car with her was her stepdaughter, who was also killed and her young son, who was injured. In the car behind them were her husband, her baby daughter and another stepson. Her husband's car was not involved in the accident. I worked with Camilla on two occasions. The first was a year after she died and the second time was about four months later. This is what happened.

I dedicated myself in prayer for good and to God. I visualized a small image of myself in my mind and asked to be with Camilla. I perceived no path so I mentally projected a beam of light, like a searchlight sweeping the sky to see if I could intersect this beam with her. The beam stopped on a dark gray energy swirl, a cloudy mass that seemed to consist of anger and frustration. I stayed with this image to see if it had anything to do with Camilla. I heard the word fury and this fury seemed to be facing me. I visualized a shield of protective light between my mind and this fury, as I didn't want any of this fury to affect me.

I didn't know if this was with Camilla, so I asked for some form or representation of Camilla to work with. I then realized she was connected to this cloudy dark mass. Camilla was keeping this fury between us because it was in the forefront of her experience. I had to get around the edge of this projection of anger to reach her.

I saw that Camilla wanted to throw this ball of fury down onto the earth. She wanted to demolish the accident site. I understood this fury was something she has had with her since the accident.

I asked Camilla if she could step away from the dark mass. She tried but the mass was still right next to her and the darkness overlapped or bled across her (memory) body. I addressed Camilla directly and said perhaps we could find a way to unload or disperse this from her. Camilla said, "I don't see any way of doing this as long as my children are down there."

I asked Camilla where she has been since she died. I got the word nebulous, that she has been caught up in the vortex of this fury and frustration. She showed me the image of herself spinning within this dark cloud, with her arms outstretched.

I asked her about what made it possible for her to understand she had died. She answered, "I heard the prayers of the people on earth for me. At first the raging storm of my emotions blocked those prayers, but the prayers reached tentacles of energy toward me and I turned some of my attention toward that energy. That energy helped get my attention away from the incredible anger of having died. The prayers gave me an alternative

211

platform to step back on and that platform is where I am staying."

I saw this platform of a neutral tan color. It had been created by the prayers of her friends and family on earth. She admitted it was not anything of her own making. I asked Camilla if she would like my help to try to get beyond the experience that has enveloped her so profoundly since her death.

Camilla answered, "I have some questions. I hope you can help me with them. I seem so isolated. When we died, I saw that my stepdaughter's death was so much more empowered than mine. She was in the light and able to advance and function. She was in a good place and understands the act of her short life and her death in terms of the greater whole of her existence. She was comfortable and well adjusted, but I am not. I am interested if you can shed any light on where I am at this point."

I suggested to Camilla that she draw whatever light and power she can into her present reality. "I know you believed in God, draw grace into yourself through prayer." Camilla said, "I don't feel as if I can do that now." I told her I'd like to try some things to help her. She moved then and put the ball of fury back between us. I focused God's love from my own point of power into the mass and infused it with crystalline white light. This seemed to dissolve the large mass, but there was still a small ball of fury that stayed in her heart area. I focused a more concentrated beam of love into the core of this mass.

As soon as I did that I got a sinking sensation, of sinking into a deeper trance state. I felt my mental vehicle and Camilla's memory body sliding downward.

212

The scene was changing around us. I prayed to continue to be with Camilla as this was the first time I had reached her. It felt like we were going down a curved slide, and I worked to keep the visualization of Camilla with me. I reached out to hold her while we made this transition. We were traveling through some dimension that I cannot really describe. All I had was a strong sense of motion. But while we were moving, her body was getting more distinct and she was crying. Camilla was releasing a lot of emotion and weeping.

The movement slowed and I still had my arms around her. We had arrived in some other place and time. My first impression was of small bushes on a grassy plane. I have the feeling this was one of Camilla's other lifetimes. Perhaps we were there to see an explanation or a pattern that will help her.

I saw that we were on a dry, grassy plane in Africa. When I looked back to Camilla I saw an extremely tall black woman, well over six feet tall. She was decorated with the most marvelous earrings, necklaces and bracelets and she was carrying a spear. I understood her to be a knowledgeable huntress. She had a very different sense of womanhood than I do.

I asked to see what, in this African life time, matches the lifetime when she was Camilla. Camilla said, "my strength, my courage and my aggressiveness as Camilla was related to this lifetime, mostly my aggressiveness." I asked her what her name was in this lifetime and she made a sound I could not translate. It was like the sound rapidly flowing water would make going around or under a big rock in a river.

I asked this African Camilla to show us what, in this lifetime, we needed to understand. An answer came that if Camilla had explored reincarnation when she was alive she would have learned what we were seeing. This African lifetime would have explained some of her powers, affinities and foibles because Camilla was such an unusual character in her life. She was sometimes aghast at her own behavior. Had she known of this lifetime it would have explained, or illustrated, aspects of her personality to her. But even now that she is deceased this psychic exploration is just as valid. All that came to me in a flash. The words took a minute to speak but the information came in a split second.

We walked from the dry, grassy plane into a village. As I looked at the village life, I got chills. The African Camilla did not have children in this lifetime. It was something denied her because of her rank and status as a huntress. It was a requirement of this high status that she could not have children. As we walked through the village I saw that the African Camilla commanded a lot of respect, and although she was not a leader, she was admired in her village.

Celibacy was a large part of the status that she had. In fact she lived in a kind of commune with other women elevated to the same status. It was quite an honor for her to be what she was.

The African Camilla was looking at the children as she walked through the village. I cannot even try to express the longing I feel she had for the children. I had chills and tears in my eyes. I asked Camilla if this was a choice that she made. She answered, "at the turn of puberty I had the choice whether to pursue this status or not. This choice was open to me because of my birth order in the tribe. I could have rejected this but it seemed very glamorous at the time. At that age (of about eleven years old) I was not interested in having babies yet. I did not realize at that young age what it would mean to not have babies as a mature woman."

I saw that the African Camilla got to be old in that life. Her ornaments changed as she got older. She had gray hair with woven banding around her forehead. The patterning of the braiding denoted high status. She was never a village official but everyone came to her because she was so wise. Now that her childbearing years were over, she was much more at peace with her choice. She had a peaceful death in that lifetime, surrounded by people who honored her on a comfortable mat. She was well cared for and simply died of old age. As her spirit left that body I took Camilla's hand and we were traveling upwards with the spirit of this deceased African woman. I thought how good it was for Camilla to have seen a natural death in this way.

We arrived at the beige disk and the feeling of movement has stopped. The spirit of the African woman had faded but Camilla's form was much more distinct to me. I asked Camilla to sit so we could talk over what just happened.

We sat facing each other, cross legged. There was a lot of emotion being released by Camilla. She said, "I have to think about that, I don't want to talk about it now." So I enveloped Camilla in love and gentleness and assured her that she was all right. I assured her that she was in a process and won't be stuck anymore. She asked where she would be now because she was tethered to the earth by that ball of fury. I told her that she can stay near the earth and close to her family. I told her that she is in her present which is her point of power. I suggested we pray for healing because she has been through such a traumatic period since she died. I assured her I would continue to pray that she reach a place of peace within herself.

I meditated again for Camilla a few months later. I returned to the beige disk, but this time it was luminous. I found her quickly and she was moving to me with her arms outstretched, happy to see me. We held each other for a moment.

She had so much more of her personality intact than when I last saw her. She had energy sparkling around her and her image was much clearer than it was before. I expressed surprise that she is still on the disk where I last met her. She said, "I need seclusion and privacy still. This suited me perfectly. I am too fragile to venture from here to do anything else."

I asked her what she has been thinking and experiencing. Camilla replies, "I have been enjoying the feeling of my body again. I am quite a bit more integrated with the sensations my body remembers. I have also been soaking up energy like sunshine."

"I have been thinking about my husband more than my children at this point, of the lost and missed opportunities. I realize more that my children are people unto themselves. I realize now that I was linked more with my husband than my children. I am sorry that I didn't see that while I was in life. I probably would have gotten to that realization sooner or later, but at the point that I died I was so enamored with my babies. I didn't see this then and I feel sad my husband is alone."

"I feel like I have been sick for a long time. Now I am getting out into the sunshine and being healthy. I am reveling in the feeling of being alive and vibrant after spending so long feeling just empty. I am now able to feel the pleasant earth type things like warmth and breezes. I have been able to feel some of the best earth experience." Camilla showed me herself dancing. She said, "my prayer took the form of dancing, through the movement of my arms and legs I was able to heal." I asked Camilla if there was anything she wanted me to tell her family and she receded just then. I get the sense she cannot cope with that concept. As she was receding into the beige light she said, "just tell them I am fine, I am really fine."

This meditation really shows how important our prayers and love are for the deceased. I shudder to think what Camilla's deceased experience would have been without so much love being sent to her after her death.

We must make every effort to send the deceased, especially suicides, murder victims, and other deceased we know who died tragically, our love and prayers. We must think of them healthy and whole. We have to hold in our mind a vision of them in a time in their life when they were happy.

Death is not a test. If the deceased do not achieve self realization and progress through the stages of the afterlife smoothly, they are not losers. Every deceased person takes an individual path to self realization, assimilation, healing and progression, unique to their personality. If the deceased set out to deliberately participate in the new reality they find themselves in, they cannot fail.

Chapter Fifteen

The Faces of Angels

"Now don't you get lost out there."

I was years into this work before I told anyone in my family that I communicated with the deceased. Of course, I told my mother first. Her immediate response was, "Now, don't you get lost out there." She went on to explain that her maternal grandmother was psychic. Before the days of electricity and telephones she said her grandmother always knew who was on their way to visit and exactly when they would arrive. My mother said her grandmother always just knew things.

Isn't it interesting what we don't know about our family? But what my mother said made sense. Her maternal grandmother, my great grandmother Drury, was the ancestor who told me essentially how the afterlife worked in a meditation. I spent many years researching the clues she gave me.

Before I was a consciously practicing medium, I was an intuitive person. I always paid attention to that certain little voice in my head warning me of, say, the presence of a policeman up ahead when I was speeding. Before caller ID I was never wrong about who was calling. Even to this day, I don't bother when I know it's a telemarketer. There probably is a genetic component to my mental ability. Like my great-grandmother, and my mother, I've always just known things.

I think intuition can be developed into some degree of psychic ability. I was an intuitive and an intensely spiritual child, praying and loving God with all my heart. I have always been close to animals. I am good at non verbal communication because I can mentally see what they visualize to me. It has always been easy for me to sense enhanced vitality in some plants, bushes, and trees. But I didn't have imaginary friends or see the deceased as a child. It was never my goal to be a psychic medium when I grew up. My work as a medium is a result of my spiritual path, not the core or purpose of my spiritual work.

At the beginning, I had to work at bringing intuitive knowledge into a deliberate conscious thought process. I began to do this the year several people who were close to me died. That year I also met the man who is now my husband. Strangely enough, we had attended the same university when we were young. I was even once in his dormitory room with a group of friends in our freshman year. He wasn't there, but I saw the photos of his horse he had tucked into the mirror over his bureau. I picked up his comb and told his roommate I wanted to meet the person the comb belonged to.

Years later we met in another part of the state. The first time I laid eyes on him I knew he was somehow important to me. We would see each other at Sierra Club meetings from time to time and chat about horses. More years would go by before I realized why we felt so connected.

I saw an advertisement for a local psychic named Kathleen Kalina. I got the idea, and eventually the nerve, to ask him to go for a past life regression. I arranged for us to go to psychics separately. Three of the lifetimes he saw matched detail for detail with three I saw. It was clear we had a history. Many more years would go by before I knew this was the owner of that comb and even more years until we started our life together.

Not long after I had my past life regression Kathleen called me and asked me to help her find her cat Chela. Kathleen asked me if I would go with her to the last campground that she had stopped in, which was about a hundred miles away. She thought perhaps Chela had escaped from her camper there. Kathleen went on to explain that she was emotionally distraught so she couldn't see where Chela was by herself. She also said she knew I was a psychic.

Kathleen's idea of me as a psychic made me nervous. I had no knowledge of any ability I had that could help her. I felt I owed it to her to try, but I had no idea about how this would happen. At that time I was not communicating with the deceased, but I was praying for them.

My deceased paternal grandmother loved cats. This grandmother had given me a cross stitched pillow with a Siamese on it that I had forgotten about. The evening after Kathleen called I was reaching for something in a closet and that pillow fairly jumped into my hands from a higher shelf. In my prayers that night I asked Granny for help. The next morning when I went outside, I found myself standing next to and touching a huge catnip plant I had grown for my own cat family.

Kathleen and I went that day and there were large catnip plants surrounding an old barn back from the road near the campground. I knew Chela was there somewhere. Although we called her, Chela did not come. I suggested we leave a sweater of Kathleen's in the barn and we left some cat food as well. The next day when Kathleen returned to the site, Chela was sitting on her sweater.

On the trip up and back Kathleen and I had a chance to talk. She told me I was gifted. My gift would influence my life choices once I accepted it and began to practice it. I was skeptical but I wanted to learn more. I began reading books by and about psychics, and collected books published by the Theosophical Society. I have always been a practical, systematic, down to earth person. Yet, I was curious. Did I have some ability in the unseen, the seemingly unprovable, intangible psychic world?

I went back to Kathleen for a life purpose reading. This time I paid attention to the process, not just the results. We started by dedicating the meditation to God and for good. Then she had me imagine a flower opening in the center of my head, just above my spine, and to imagine my spine as a column of energy. She said to make a small image of my body, to imagine this image sitting in the center of the flower with the energy of my spine washing up over it. She suggested I envision a path for the small image of myself to follow to a spiritual house. After I described my imaginary house, she had me go inside and look for the book of my life, where I could look at my past, present and possible future choices.

I still use the visualization of my small self, which I now know represents my mind. It is my mental vehicle. I change my mental focus by repeating the simple prayer: God is love and he who abides in love abides in God and God in him. Often, the small image of myself is encapsulated in a protective sphere before I leave the center of the flower in order to reach more distant energy levels. I believe this sphere is formed by the angelic energy that I sense is often present in my life. The path

224

I follow takes many different forms. I am careful to retrace the path back to my physical body.

I am now comfortable with this mental duality, this multitasking with my mind. I was impressed when my second cousin, who died as a young adult in a car accident, saw me sitting in my chair in my home and also sitting in a chair on a porch in a mental environment his grandmother had constructed so we could talk. In all the years I have been doing the work no deceased person had ever asked how I could seem to be in two places at once. I was impressed by his ability to see this.

The core of my ability is not just being able to concentrate well enough to see and hear the deceased. I'd bet there are many mediums more gifted than I am. Discernment, which means a sensitivity to the truth of an intangible event, is my real gift. I don't think I am unusual because I know when the police are out with a speed trap, who is going to call me today, if an errand will not pan out, or that I can speak with the deceased. If I have a gift, it is being able to tell knowing from imagining. This quality of intuition is validated when I see the speed trap, the expected phone call does come in, I learn the store did close early, and if I am in the present with the deceased.

Before I was confident that I was in real time with the deceased, and not just imagining the conversations, I practiced with the deceased I had known in life. This was a safe way to explore. My ancestors were tremendously helpful and cooperative. Eventually I could speak what I was seeing and hearing into a tape recorder. It didn't matter what I saw or heard at that time. I was just getting my wings. But things got interesting quickly.

Camilla, in the chapter on Soul Rescue, was the very first person outside my own family I contacted. Camilla and her stepdaughter's deaths were such a tragedy in my circle of friends. My only goal in that meditation was to pray for her and give her my love. I had no intention of ever sharing my fledgling work with her family. Eventually I did, with trepidation, pass on the transcript of Camilla's meditation to her family. Camilla's mother let me know that she felt I had reached and been with Camilla.

At first I couldn't remember much of what went on in my prayers for the dead as they took the form of meditations with the deceased. When I transcribed my audio tape with Camilla, not only did I not remember what went on but I also had no reference point to understand what had transpired. My ignorance only fueled my desire to understand more. I am a person who wants to know how things work.

When I ran out of dead friends and ancestors to talk to, I knew I had to venture further afield. It was a nerve-wracking decision to expose my ability, or possibly lack of it, to other people. What I saw was so detailed that it could only be true or false. When I described the placement of the window to the couch, the fabric on the couch, the way the deceased appeared to me right down to their shoes, it felt like truth or consequences. Being a medium is an exacting task. There is no way I can research or know ahead of time the details I see.

I also envied the psychics I read about who have a spirit guide bringing them information, or intervening so the chosen deceased could be contacted. What a

226

comfort it would be to depend on another persona for the work. Don't get me wrong- I know I have help. I do feel protected when I am out of body, but I do not see a guide when I meditate. It was explained to me once that we are a tiny link in a chain of angels, made of the same starlight or essence reaching all the way from God/Source to earth. Our guides and guardian angels are actually a higher form of the same being that we are. I think the energy of my being forms the sphere that encapsulates me when I mentally travel.

I meditated for living friends at first. I never took money for the meditations, as that implied a contract. Besides, money would have made me more anxious about the work. I didn't understand where and how I was reaching the deceased for a few years. I didn't understand why there were times when it didn't work. When it didn't work, I wanted to know why. However, it worked much more than it didn't, and gradually I started to trust. I kept myself surrounded by the light of God's love and kept practicing.

The beginning years of this work were hard times in my personal life. Perhaps the stress of that time enhanced my creative drive. Looking back, I know I had to gather some self esteem to make some life changes. Nothing I had accomplished in life so far made me feel worthy. This work was my own, my gift. I was ambitious with this work in a way that I had never been with anything else I'd accomplished. For the first time in my life I felt like the universe approved of me and loved me. I felt unique.

Then I realized that, although I could speak with the deceased, I did not yet have the maturity to be a counselor to the living. I did not have the tools to help the living process the emotion that resulted by my communication with their deceased loved ones. I was in a much different emotional place with the deceased than my living clients were. I could empathize with the living, but I was not a therapist.

At the beginning I was always more interested in helping the deceased than the living. Eventually, I understood the framework of the steps and stages of the afterlife. However, every deceased's experience of the afterlife was so different. Just because I understood exactly where they were their experience didn't mean the deceased understood where they were in their experience. So far, I have spent more time explaining the afterlife to the deceased than to the living.

The living continued to be a problem for me. How do I tell a friend whose father was a lifelong alcoholic that he is not self knowing and I can't reach him? How can I tell a mother her beloved child really committed suicide, that the death was not an accident? How do I tell a father that his daughter is not missing, she was murdered? At times I knew I was in way over my head. The logical next step would have been to become affiliated with a therapist or grief counselor.

Then, in middle age, I initiated a major life change. I walked away from all that I had built, all that was familiar, the land and most of the animals that I loved. I started life over. My work took a back seat until I came out of the other side of that personal Armageddon.

I now sit finishing this book more than twenty years into the work. My life is different now. We are also at a different point in the spiritual evolution of our species.

The role of psychic mediums used to be to prove the existence of the deceased. People wanted case by case proof of the afterlife. Now, many of us accept that the afterlife exists. A valid medium can still help ease the suffering of the separation of the living and the deceased, client by client. Detailed messages prove our loved ones still exist.

At this juncture in our history, however, we need to understand how we will feel, function and progress after we die. The study of death is not about someone else anymore. This book is not about the deceased. We need the information that will give us the courage to face our own death transition and all that this understanding means to the time we have left in life. The understanding of death will also help us in the grieving process when we lose a loved one.

I had a variety of people read this manuscript before it was published. Most of the readers said the book was a comfort to them. I think it is a comfort to know at least some of what we can expect in the afterlife. If we have less fear of what happens after death it makes it easier for us to accept our mortality.

My hope is that this book will also be a comfort to those who have lost a loved one. I pray for the parents tragically separated from their children by death. For them grief is not a process but a burden they cannot ever put aside. If I ever have to limit my practice it will be for parents who lose children of any age. I hope this book is a comfort to the families effected by the evil wars and by 9/11. Collective grief is the only response we have to these events of great magnitude. But even as we grieve these tragedies we can know we will see our children, husbands, or parents again. Although the time of our separation seems long and is painful, our reunion is something we can look forward to.

The study of death has made me extremely aware of my time in life, particularly the time I hope to have left. A young horse I bred will be in his twenties when I am in my seventies. Do I have twenty more years to garden or ride? Do I have the time in life to fulfill my life's intent and accomplish what I planned to do before I was born? If I really lived in my present would I have all the time in the world or be outside of time like the deceased?

The afterlife is a completely self directed mental and spiritual reality. What if we lived our life as if life was a completely self directed reality as well? Of course we are immersed in the physical laws as our physical body is part of this system or level of energy. And we are vulnerable to evil here. But what if our mind and spirit, our LOVE determined our reality here? I'm beginning to believe the mind and spirit do eventually bring the reality we imagine into the physical experience we live within.

I can't help but compare aspects of the afterlife to physical life. One summer evening I was driving through a local small town and the townspeople had gathered for a band concert. The setting sun gilded the children, parents, dogs, flowers and grass. In that moment I knew that whole scene and experience could be a recreated in the future in the city of light. Or perhaps those people had explored small town New England life in the human species consciousness pool, then in life sought to re-create and participate in a similar experience here. The way we communicate and learn at the human species consciousness pool is identical to electronic communication here without the gadgets. I often see that mirroring or duality of experiences between earthly life and the afterlife.

I admit I have an odd relationship with the grim reaper. There really are elements of the afterlife I am looking forward to. The first thing I will do is skim over our hay fields. I want to fly like the birds that eat the bugs our haying equipment kicks up when we are making hay. When I get to the human species consciousness pool I want to explore North and South America when only native people lived there. I will be able to see the farm my ancestors lived on that is all a sub-division now. I thought these times were lost forever. I don't believe they are anymore. It is all stored in the human species consciousness pool and in my ancestor's memory. I know it will be possible to have some experience of this history in inter lifetime.

And yet as I write this a dear, dear friend is fighting a battle with cancer. Dotte and her husband began their life together the very same month and year as my husband and I did. For either one of us to only have a little more than a decade within our second marriages is a tragedy too sad to contemplate. And even though I know I will be able to continue our friendship mentally if she dies, her illness brings my focus back to the preciousness of time in life here.

Dotte has been both a friend and one of my personal human angels, protecting and encouraging me in my life. I consider some of the deceased I have communicated with over the years also as my personal angels. They were angels to trust me and tell me what they knew.

Some deceased stayed with me for prolonged periods while I acknowledged them and prayed with them. Some have come to comfort me, like the grandmother of the family in the beginning of Chapter 8 who I felt with me once, when I cried months after my mother died. I knew some of these people before they died, some became friends as we got to know each other in the meditations. I felt their anger at being murdered, their joy at being out of pain, their confusion at not knowing where to turn next. I validated their existence. They validated my gift. Coming face to face with these angels again after I die will be a pleasure.

Kathleen, the first psychic I ever met, proved to be right about one other thing. Emotions can cause mental static. So much so, that psychics cannot work for themselves. The first Christmas after my mother died, I felt her essence near me. Later, I attempted conscious communication with her. But I could tell early into the meditation that I was reading a memory and was not with her in our mutual present. I am hoping that, in time and with healing, communication will be possible for us. What a joy it will be to come face to face with her once again whenever that happens . There is no angel I would rather be with, no face I would rather see again.

Appendices

Where We Can Be in the Afterlife

The Death Transition
Occurs on the surface of the earth

The Near-earth Deceased Experience
Occurs parallel to our earth experience

Completion of the Prior Life
Occurs after the earth portal transition
which leads to healing energy levels

The Threshold of Choice
A transition area where the choice to ascend or to
remain within the circle of life is made.

Inter Lifetime
Occurs at the Human Species Consciousness Pool
also called the City of Light

Ascension
Unification with all other ascending life forms
including formerly animate and inanimate forms,
self knowing and non self knowing individuals.

Higher Spheres of Experience
It is logical that experience continues in realms we
cannot or do not have direct knowledge of.

What We Can Do in the Afterlife

Self Realization is identifying our self, what our personality and self-hood consist of, as we drop the physical body at death and continue to participate in more energized levels of experience. It is the first requirement for having and making choices in the afterlife.

Assimilation is translating experience into knowledge. It includes processing the events of our life and death, sorting through them for knowledge so we can make better choices. Assimilation also leads to knowing what is and what is not possible as we move into the more energized levels of the afterlife.

Healing is drawing in energy in order to make a positive change in our self. By accessing healing energy in the afterlife we improve or enhance our emotional memory, projected body or our mental and spiritual outlook. Healing is an ongoing choice in the afterlife.

Progression is a deliberate choice to move forward into different experiences or onward into more energized states of being in the afterlife. Progression may be as simple as improving our environment in the afterlife, or as profound as the undertaking of significant energy transitions to different levels of experience.

Glossary of Terms

The Afterlife is the period from physical death to inter lifetime.

Ascension is the journey back to God/Source, an eternity of ecstatic unification with all other forms of manifestation that are also ascending.

Assimilation is translating experience into knowledge; the mental or emotional digestion of life's events and relationships.

Body is the vehicle for the personality while in the physical level of experience.

Choice is an act of will by a personality.

The City of Light is another name for the human species consciousness pool where we experience inter lifetime.

A Conscious Death is when a personality is aware and can remember every aspect of events preceding their death, their actual death transition, and events surrounding their death.

Consolers are helpers at the human species consciousness pool who guide learning.

Death is a transition of a personality from the physical level of experience to a nonphysical level of experience.

Descend is to foster ignorance in the personality by repetitive acts of evil.

Earth Portal is a layer of connective energy surrounding the earth crossed both before birth and after death.

Empowerment is drawing in God/Source energy through prayer.

Euthanasia is assisting a personality in their choice to transition out of physical.

Evil is the act of destroying energy or any energy form.

Figureheads are the representatives of themes of learning at the human species consciousness pool.

Focusing Visualizations are created in the mind of the dying as the personality separates from the physical body.

Ghost is a deceased person who is unable to transit the earth portal and move on from the close proximity to the earth.

God/Source is the origin of all manifestation and the final destination for all of manifestation.

Greeters are previously deceased humans who aid the deceased when they first progress into non physical energy levels.

Guides are beings who serve to aid people both on earth and in the afterlife; also thought of as guardian angels.

Healing is drawing in energy in order to improve any condition.

Hibernation is the profound rest possible at the plane of conceptual reality.

Hub City is one of the names for the human species consciousness pool.

Human Species Consciousness Pool is where the past, present and future of the human species, from all places where humans have, are, and will ever exist, is stored and available to learn from. It is where we spend prolonged periods in between physical lifetimes.

Human is our species identity.

Inter Lifetime is the period following the afterlife and before pre-birth focus is chosen.

Levels of Experience are the energies we participate in before, in and after life.

Meditation is the creative process used to affect a change of awareness in our mind.

Memory Body is the holographic image projected by the mind of the deceased of the physical body they had at any age.

Mind is the vehicle of self knowingness.

Near-earth Experience is the period after physical death and before the deceased transit the earth portal.

Near Death Experience is when a personality begins the death transition but does not complete it.

Out of Body is when the mental vehicle is in a different location than the physical body is, whether in life or after death.

Paired or Shared Lifetime is the observation of a life on earth by a personality in inter lifetime to the exclusion of other experiences in order to learn as much as possible from the observed lifetime.

Personality is the individual intangible dynamic combination of mind and spirit.

Physical is the manifesting level for humans who choose a lifetime on earth.

Plane of Conceptual Reality/ Heavens is the level beyond the earth portal where the prior life is completely healed and assimilated.

Prayer is drawing in God/Source energy and also can be transferring this God/Source energy to anything else.

Pre-Birth Focus is when the choice for a subsequent lifetime begins to be energized by a personality.

Predeceased are the people who died before we do.

Prior Life for the deceased is the most recent life they lived on earth.

Progression is moving toward more energized experiences and possibilities in the afterlife.

Projected Environments are mentally created thought constructions resembling environments on earth.

Psychic is a person who can consciously access intuitive knowledge.

Reincarnation is the choice for a subsequent life on earth.

Self Willed Death is the mental action of relinquishing a physical body.

Self Realization is the understanding of what we are in our present.

Soul Rescue is an intervention to increase the possible choices for a personality after death.

Spirit or Soul is the God/Source component of the personality and is the receptor God/Source energy.

Suicide is the self-inflicted physical separation of the personality from the physical body.

Thought Construction is a projected mental environment that can be created at any stage of the afterlife.

The Threshold of Choice is the transition point from the plane of conceptualized heaven.

Transcendence is experiencing the eternal.

(The) **Underworld** is levels of diminished energy extending through both life and the afterlife.

The sculptural images in <u>Choices in the Afterlife</u>
by Lynne Parzini

The sculpted figures pictured in this book, some so ethereal that they seem to float off the page, others solidly earthbound and comforting, were all created in the Manhattan atelier of Rochette and Parzini. I am fortunate to be a granddaughter of Michaele Parzini, one of the founders of that studio and a dear friend of Gretchen's.

The once venerable studio of Rochette and Parzini was established in 1904 by an adventuresome duet of European sculptors. My grandfather was a handsome and expressive Italian from Turin and his partner was the more conservative, Gallic, Rochette. They met at the Beaux Arts in Paris and set out from there into an exciting future.

The two enjoyed brief acclaim and relative wealth in South America only to be displaced by political upheaval. Their move to New York City was fortuitous. The studio that they established at 215 E 25th Street attracted churchmen, architects and wealthy private citizens seeking classical sculptural adornment for homes, churches, businesses and institutions.

Although the studio does not exist anymore, one may see some of their stunning work today on or in important buildings all over the country. For example, the bronze doors of St. Patrick's Cathedral, the facade of St. John the Divine, the ornamentation in the Waldorf Astoria and at the New York Amphitheater were produced by Rochette and Parzini. To paraphrase a lovely song lyric, they put many an angel into the architecture.

The soaring heroic rendering of the heaven bound man and woman was inspired by a small Gladys Vanderbuilt Whitney original. The sculpture that is depicted on the cover of this book, was executed in plaster of Paris and sheathed with platinum leaf. It was called the Spirit of Flight and was displayed at the 1939 World's Fair. The entire sculpture was 50 feet high, the wings were 20 feet in height, the human figures 11 feet tall. In some books on the 1939 Worlds Fair, I have seen that exhibit credited to Gertrude Vanderbuilt Whitney. However, my Aunt Lydia remembers being a young woman and standing with Gladys at the opening of the World's Fair. Aunt Lydia assures me Gladys was the designer.

My father worked with his father at the studio and took me there from time to time. The ceilings of the studio were very high in order to accommodate the execution of the tallest statues. Full size models of the sculptures were often hung on pulleys from the ceiling. I remember the sensation of seeing diaphanous beings hovering far above. These beings seemed protective of the artists below. The artists spoke in the lively cadence of their homelands while carving marble, molding clay and shaping plaster saints and sinners.

Gretchen knew my parents and was familiar with my father's and grandfather's work as I have some small pieces in my home. She asked to see my collection of the studio books consisting of photographs of various sculptures and friezes. As we looked through them she found the expression of spiritual themes executed in stone resonated perfectly with the ideas in her book. This happy collaboration honors my father and grandfather's work, Gretchen's gift and our decades of friendship.

Author's note:
The images on the chapter title pages are there for decorative reasons only. Please don't waste time trying to figure out what the images mean or how the images are connected to the text.

Choices in the Afterlife, Summary

The good news about the afterlife is that we are not different people after we die. The bad news about the afterlife is that we are not different people after we die. We begin the afterlife with the same sense of humor, coping skills, memories, attitudes, intelligence, reverence and spiritual beliefs that we had in life.

No matter how they arrive at the knowledge, the deceased have to realize that they are still themselves, although out of the physical body they identified so strongly with in life. Their afterlife begins when the deceased are conscious and functioning without their body. I call this process self realization. It is the first task for the newly deceased. No choices can be made until self realization is achieved.

Assimilation is the next task or process the deceased enact. Assimilation means thinking about experience and translating that experience into knowledge. The deceased review their life. They mentally digest and distill both the good parts and the hard events of their life. They think about the beliefs and attitudes that governed their choices in life.

Healing is yet another activity for the deceased. Healing takes place in several ways. In the process of self realization, the deceased can achieve healing from the manner of their death. Assimilation leads to healing from the difficulties of life. Healing also takes place when the deceased learn to empower and energize themselves in the afterlife.

The fourth process the deceased participate in is progression. It is easy to measure our progression in terms of

245

age in life. We are carried along by the river of time. But the deceased are outside of time. Progression for the deceased is the process of improving their reality by increasing the knowledge of their choices. Progression is striving toward better situations and more mental and spiritual possibilities in the afterlife.

The deceased enact these four, somewhat overlapping activities, self realization, assimilation, healing and progression, in a series of energy levels. We can think of these levels of energy as places. This is the way we are able to understand them.

When we die, we don't go anywhere at first. We stay near the earth. If we retain consciousness throughout the death transition, we are present and observe our own wake and funeral rituals. No matter when we achieve awareness or self realization we stay near familiar people and places until we become oriented to our new reality. I call this level or "place" the near-earth deceased experience.

After death, we remember what it was like to be in a body. The deceased carry this memory in their mind. This memory is like an echo of the body. It is projected by the deceased as a holographic image in the size and shape of the body that they had in life. I call this mental projection the memory body. To the deceased, the memory body seems to be interpreting information and defining their self image in the same way that their physical body did in life. I can perceive this thought projection of their body when I meditate with the deceased.

Death was a transition from the physical to the near-earth deceased experience. When the deceased have accomplished all the self realization, assimilation and healing they wish to near the earth, they choose to make another transition. The next transition moves the deceased away from the earth. This transition changes the way they can perceive and interact with the earth's energy.

I call this further transition phenomenon the earth portal. The earth portal is connective energy that encircles our planet much like the atmosphere. We transit this connective energy coming into physical at birth and leaving the close proximity to the planet at some point after death. The earth portal is perceived as grayish because, of itself, it has no energy for us to use or accumulate. The deceased do not linger in the earth portal. This is a transitional area only.

I think of the level of energy beyond the earth portal as the plane of conceptual reality. I wish I had a shorter, less complicated description. But that mouthful of words describes what is possible for the deceased in this plane of experience. In this level light and color are malleable and the deceased can easily form or shape beautiful realities for themselves. Since there is no pre-existing landscape here, the deceased have to create environments to be within. These imaginary realities often resemble beautiful places they have lived in or visited on earth. These individual environments are thought projections created by the deceased.

The deceased create personal realities here in order to perform profoundly solitary assimilation and healing work. The abundance of energy at this level also makes total healing from physical life possible. Here, the deceased become increasingly objective and detached from their prior life. Individual work at this level can take as long as needed or desired. When the deceased feel they have completely healed and assimilated their prior life, they become aware of yet another place or level that beckons to them.

247

The deceased become aware of a void at the edge of the plane of conceptual reality. Across the void they perceive a city of light gleaming off in the distance. This city of light is the human species consciousness pool. They do not have to know what this place is. The appeal of the city will draw their attention. The deceased cross the void to the city by simply concentrating on the light.

The city of light is the level of energy where all of human experience, from every time period, from every culture, on every theme, from everywhere humans have ever existed is stored and available to learn about. The deceased here can mentally experience anything they wish to for as long as they wish. In addition, the City of Light is a social level of experience where humans communicate with each other, share memories, and explore knowledge and themes both individually and in groups. Many deceased think this is heaven, but the city of light is not heaven.

Ascension is the heaven of our religions. Ascension is an eternity of ecstatic unification with people and other life forms who are also in the process of ascension. In the simplest of terms, everything leaves God/Source with a general intent, what of God we will attempt to manifest on earth. When we feel that this intent is completely expressed on earth, our return to God/Source becomes an abiding and conscious goal in physical life. We will not have the knowledge of and therefore the choice for ascension in the afterlife unless ascension was a conscious goal that governed our lifetime.

Ascension can be chosen and enacted at any time after death. The choice to ascend and ultimately merge with God/Source results in the end of self knowledge. It is the end of our individuality. That is why some deceased who know ascension is a choice they can make, and who energized this choice in physical life, still choose to postpone ascension in the afterlife. These ascending deceased can choose to linger near the earth, in the plane of conceptual reality or at the city of light.

The deceased who are not aware of the choice for ascension will naturally gravitate to the city of light. They are now in what I call inter-lifetime. Inter lifetime is a phase where the deceased have finished working on their prior life and are not yet focused on the next step. This next step can be the choice to incarnate into a successive lifetime on earth.

There are deceased who flounder in the afterlife. Some are mentally caught up in the profound emotions they carried with them into death. Others never experienced love or awe during life and simply don't know how to make positive choices in the afterlife. Still others have chosen to diminish or even annihilate their spiritual nature through consistent acts of evil in life.

My private meditation work is with the deceased who are not functioning well. This is called soul rescue. I work with struggling deceased in meditation to influence their thinking toward something positive, and if possible, toward God/Source. I try to move them to a better mental focus where they can begin to assimilate and heal from their prior life. My public meditation work bridges the gap between the living and the deceased provides a degree of solace for grieving loved ones.

Updates 2009

I have been able to contact my mother in trance state several times. In one of these emotional conversations she said that we have not had any other lifetimes together before- this was our first, and that I would have come in through whoever my father had married. This was an oddly comforting thing to learn and felt right as it is my father and I that had work and learning to do with each other in this lifetime. On a lighter note, she also asked me to take some of the chicken manure from our flock of hens, and fertilize her flower gardens that surround the home where my father still lives. Her flowers are blooming happily this summer.

Dotte and I have (mentally) chatted several times. It was her idea that I should start doing my trance readings for bereaved clients over the telephone. I was not sure I could stay in trance state while interacting with a living client, but it turned out that I can. See the Solace Medium Service page in HowSpiritWorks.com if you are interested in a reading. I now have developed an interactive form of the meditations where my living clients get to mentally touch the energy of their deceased loved ones. It is wonderful for parents and children.

I am listed in the A.R.E. (The Edgar Cayce Foundation) catalog. I'm grateful for their enthusiasm about my book. I have national distribution and Amazon sales have been, well, amazing.

I continue to meet the most delightful deceased people in the readings. I plan to look some of them up when I am out of physical. I have a newsletter that goes out about once a month with new things I have learned from working with the deceased. If you wish to receive it please email me through my site, HowSpiritWorks.com.

This book was also translated and published in French. September of 2009, Le Dauphin Blanc published: Les Choix Dans l'au-Dela. I am now getting wonderful letters in French and thank God for translation tools. The book was translated by Sylvie Oulette, who is also a metaphysical author. One day I hope to place this book with Hay House, so if any of you readers have an in, let's network.

I decided to do a new edition as my thinking has evolved in some areas. I wish I could have included more stories in this second edition as the deceased continue to give me different perspectives about this life on earth.

I am currently studying Eva Pierrakos, an advanced pure channel who worked from 1950 to the late 70s. Her unedited transcripts can be downloaded from International Pathway Foundation. Fear No Evil is a book based on her meditations. I also listen to the tapes of Esther Hicks channeling Abraham, she makes me laugh. The music of Snatam Kaur nourishes my soul. The tools I use change as I progress on my spiritual path.

I appreciate the comments I receive from readers and I also have a fan page on Facebook for friends and visitors.

Thanks to all of you who have honored me with your time and attention to my book.

INDEX

Acknowledgments

My gratitude goes to these dear friends and family that helped me with this book.

Heather Adler for proofing the second edition. Barbara Lanteigne for typing the first versions eons ago and invaluable criticism and support, over and over, as the book took shape, Beth Cote for your big heartedness to read ideas so foreign to you, Carl Lanteigne for technical support, Joe Tolman at Bulldog Designs in Keene, NH for the cover design, John Vogel for teaching me to format in Word Perfect, Lynne Parzini for your irreplaceable contribution to the artistic theme of the book and your contemplative suggestions, Matt Saxton who finished the editing, Peter Vogel for your generosity, Ray David for his professional advice, Sy Montgomery for always believing in me as a writer, Kim Guarnaccia, for helping to solve the distribution riddle. If I have forgotten anyone please let me know, your omission was not intentional.

My thanks also goes to the many deceased individuals who contributed to this work. Even though I have changed your names to honor the privacy of your families, I hope you are pleased with your contribution to this book.

My thanks to Dotte McDonald David who told me, after she died, that reading my book completely removed her fear as she was dying. That made all my work on this book worth it. Dotte, you are so missed.

Most of all, my gratitude goes to my husband and spiritual mate for your support and for sharing this adventure called life with me once again.

Contact Information

HowSpiritWorks.com~Website
Howspiritworksdotcom ~YouTube
Howspiritworks ~Facebook
gretchenv@howspiritworks.com

I am not doing personal readings at
this time, thank you

Gretchen Vogel

Choices Publishing
Keene, NH

"A must-read for all spiritual truth-seekers."
Kim Guarnaccia, editor,Mysteries Magazine

"Call me crazy, but Gretchen Vogel's sincerity and courage in writing about her life's mission (at the risk that some might call her crazy) didn't just give me pause, it brought me to a full stop. What if?"
Rebecca Rule, syndicated columnist

"I recommend this book to all my mortal friends"
Sy Montgomery, author

"Congratulations on your brave and articulate book"
Steve Sherman, book reviewer
for the Keene (H) Sentinel

"(this)Writers sincerity challenges even the skeptical"
Concord (NH) Monitor"

262